OK, LET'S TALK ABOUT IT
Dynamics of Dialogue

OK, LET'S TALK ABOUT IT

Dynamics of Dialogue

CATHRINA BAUBY

 VAN NOSTRAND REINHOLD COMPANY

NEW YORK CINCINNATI TORONTO LONDON MELBOURNE

Van Nostrand Reinhold Company Regional Offices:
New York Cincinnati Chicago Millbrae Dallas

Van Nostrand Reinhold Company International Offices:
London Toronto Melbourne

Copyright © 1972 by Litton Educational Publishing, Inc.

Library of Congress Catalog Card Number: 72-4174
ISBN: 0-442-20598-8

Manufactured in the United States of America

Published by Van Nostrand Reinhold Company
450 West 33rd Street, New York, N.Y. 10001

Published simultaneously in Canada by Van Nostrand Reinhold Ltd.

15 14 13 12 11 10 9 8 7 6 5 4 3 2 1

To G. Bauby

Preface

"I didn't understand," is one of the most costly sentences in modern business. Through research, interviews, and role playing conducted with a cross section of business and industry groups throughout the United States, I report: It's a breakdown in dialogue that causes much of the expensive dissention, indecision, and *wrong* decision making in business. Both executive experience and formal research have proved repeatedly that, on the job, approximately 90% of the failures are due to a breakdown in successful communications with other people. Only 10% of the failures are due to a lack of technical skills.

How then can we decrease job dissatisfaction and increase work proficiency? It's reasonable to conclude that those who learn and *practice* effective dialogue will have found the answer to these questions. Through employing effective dialogue creativity can be tapped, problem solving expedited, and understanding between employer and employee heightened. By acquaintance with and application of the dynamics of dialogue, we can reduce tensions on the job, in our personal lives, and socially. The process begins with people saying, "OK, let's talk about it."

How have we learned to dialogue? We've learned to dialogue through our association with family, friends, and the environment into which we were born.

Our parents were the first to influence us. We listened to their words, their tones and their phrasing. We were told that children should be seen and not heard, so we were quiet. Or siblings influenced us. We may have been quieted by them, or teased and taught defensive dialogue. As we circulated into the sphere outside the family, we learned the rhetoric of our peers and teachers with whom we associated. We were influenced by the customs of our society. If we traveled with a "tough talking group," our dialogue might have been that of the street gang. If we were early-trained in elocution, chances are we learned the language of eloquent facade.

We exhibited the extremes of the scale of dialogue, or our words fell some place in between. We defended ourselves either by speaking up or by shutting up. We learned to express our thinking verbally, or not at all. We learned to verbalize respect or to hide it, to shout or to be silent. Our environment stimulated us to be talkers or listeners, or a combination of both. It provoked our dialogue to be pithy or tempered with tact. We were conditioned to verbalize feelings or to keep them to ourselves. These were early patterns of childhood. In infancy, we established the dialogical format for our future. This format is not always desirable, nor is it always effective.

As we move away from family, friends, and community, into the world of work, suddenly, we're thrown into a new environment. Here we deal with new people—new experiences. We bring with us from our youth culture the basic elements of interpersonal communications. Some adapt for us and are acceptable. Others are ineffectual and nonfunctional. They must be replaced with new dialogical techniques. These must be pertinent to the contemporary world of business. Where then, do we learn these techniques for effective dialogue?

In high school, I took *all* of the speech courses offered. They were public speaking, and public speaking. Speech was my undergraduate major in college. The department offered a broad spectrum of courses. These ran the gamut from public speaking, debate and drama—to acting and announcing—to lighting, stagecraft, and directing. Yet, no where in that or any other department, was *any* course offered on *people talking to people*—DIALOGUE.

For 18 years I have been a professional speaker in the business world. I have addressed thousands of audiences, in size from 5 to 5000. Six years ago, through feedback from my audiences, I began realizing, as did others, the old bromide course, public speaking, wasn't breaking the business communications barrier. I began looking for the ingredients missing from the traditional speech books and courses. Where were the energizers and the forces of dialogue—the things that allowed for understanding between people on a one to one basis? Amazingly, I found this area had virtually no reference material. Had no one assembled the vital elements involved in dialogue? Could it be done? Would this be a breakthrough? As I pieced together five years of research, a pattern began evolving.

First, there was an imperative need to establish what the goal of dialogue should be. Second, what comprised the component parts? Third, what are the aims of dialogue? This study became Phase I of the book, the "Semantics of Dialogue."

Research revealed the psychological factors involved in good dialogue. Further, in order to solve problems and to accomplish understanding, these psychological factors must be understood and applied. This became Phase II, the "Energizers of Dialogue."

Next, it became evident that in all meaningful dialogue, the same basic factors are at work. These elements, indigenous to all conversation, therefore became Phase III, the "Forces of Dialogue."

Together, the semantics, energizers, and forces of dialogue, when properly implemented, are the vehicle for more effective interpersonal communications.

Dialogue begins with a sentence such as "OK, let's talk about it." *Effective dialogue* continues with knowing and using the dynamics involved therein.

C.B.

Contents

PHASE III FORCES OF DIALOGUE

MEMORANDUM

TO: The Reader
FROM: Cathrina Bauby
DATE: Today
RE: Understanding *OK Let's Talk About It*

We've talked since we were two, but has anyone established guidelines on how to dialogue more effectively? This text is intended to help you make your dialogue pay off.

Dynamics of Dialogue is directed primarily to the manager. It is directed to you—from top management to line—and to those people with whom you work, with whom you associate, and with whom you live. Through reading this book, employees can better understand their managers, and wives can have better comprehension of their husband's business problems.

Regarding the case studies it presents, all have actually happened, and all participants have undergone changes in identity. While reading the cases, intersperse yourself in the roles. Think out what you'd do in a similar circumstance. It could happen to you tomorrow.

The case studies are presented as TV commercials—much happens in a brief span of time. Some of the incidents might require weeks or months to accomplish in real life. Here they're presented in a few words, succinctly, cursorily, but conclusively. The case dialogue is written in the idiom of the character involved in each specific role.

There are no pat answers to any of the cases offered; there are no pat answers in real life. Each case could have a different alternate approach, depending on the circumstances and the individuals.

OK, LET'S TALK ABOUT IT
Dynamics of Dialogue

Semantics
of
Dialogue

DIMENSIONS OF DIALOGUE

Why should today's managers, and those of tomorrow, be interested in the dimensions of dialogue?

Managers should be interested in the dimensions of dialogue, both theoretically and operationally, to enable them to be more effective achievers in executing management through people.

What's the payoff for managers—in both bottom-line numbers or dollars, and the achievement and participation of their employees?

When used effectively, dialogue is a main avenue by which management can maximize its promise or potential as well as increase its profits.

Operationally, how does this happen?

Dialogue is a vehicle to:

1. unleash the creative thinking of employees, associates, and customers;
2. create a more virile and comfortable working environment;
3. increase understanding and decrease turnover;
4. establish a fertile atmosphere for self-motivation;
5. stimulate and sustain interpersonal relationships and communications;
6. activate participative management;
7. uncover problems and discover causes;
8. clarify and verify roles, relationships, and responsibilities;
9. temper tempers and expose subjective judgments to more rational considerations; and
10. chart a joint course of action for the manager and the managed.

OK. This being the promise of dialogue—that it can do these things for management—what is dialogue and what are the dimensions of its dynamics?

Fundamentally, dialogue is participative in nature. It's the interplay of thoughts and feelings in a free flow of conversation *between* two or more people. Its basic goal is a better understanding of the needs and problems of people; its end result, problem prevention and problem solving. Its opposite is monologue. Monologue is authoritative in nature. It's one person speaking *to* another, allowing for little, if any, response on the part of the receiver, with the end result that problems still exist. *Dialogue is participative, monologue is authoritative.*

Let's look at first a monologist in action and then the dialogist in action.

Case Study No. 1 / What's Wrong?

Phillip Dalton, president of a new manufacturing company of about seventy-five employees, has called a meeting of three of his key managers to discuss an important matter requiring action.

Mr. Dalton: Good morning, gentlemen. As my memo indicated, I am concerned with the absenteeism among our employees. As I looked at the attendance record yesterday, I realized that absenteeism is a critical problem for us. It is my decision that there will be a bulletin issued to be published in quantity, and put into each of our employees' pay envelopes next week. This bulletin will inform them that they will be docked a full day's pay for each day they are absent without a doctor's written explanation. I consider this the only solution possible to impress on them that they can't just take off whenever they want to. I will appreciate your conveying this message to your employees verbally after the notice has been issued in their pay envelopes. I felt it was a matter that you should know about before the employees. I will appreciate your cooperation in enforcing my decision. That's all for now. Let's get back to work.

PROBLEM

This is a dictatorial management approach. It's classically authoritarian and totally a monologue. The problem is the lack of dialogue.

Let's take the same situation and see how it would be handled as dynamic dialogue and what the outcome would be. Al, Fred, and Smitty are Phil Dalton's key managers.

ALTERNATE APPROACH

Phil: Good morning! I see you all got my memo about a need to discuss an important matter. I was pretty vague in saying it that way, "an important matter," but I'm not sure what our problem is. I'll kick off with what triggered my feeling for a meeting, quick! I was looking at the attendance sheets. There's a high degree of absenteeism. This isn't just a flu-bug week. This has been going on for several weeks now. Could I have your thinking about what's causing this?

Fred: You're right, Phil. Smitty, Al, and I have noticed the same problem. We were talking about it again yesterday and discovered several possible reasons for this absenteeism.

Al: We did a survey of local factories and discovered that we're paying our people less than the prevailing rate. I'd suggest we consider a possible pay increase for the employees.

Smitty: I agree with Al on the pay part of it. But there are other things I've found. There are a couple of guys who seem to have some gripes about facilities. They're catalysts in the group. If they're unhappy, it seems to affect the whole group. I think we should talk with them. They're in my department, so I'll meet with them and get back to you.

Phil: That's interesting. I didn't know about either of these problems. So, wages may be a factor, and low morale due to facilities. Have you come up with anything else that can be affecting attendance?

Smitty: Yes, I've got one more thing to throw into the hopper. We've been so busy growing, I think we've failed to develop a team spirit with our people. Maybe we should put out a weekly bulletin about what's happening with us internally, and with our people. Maybe we can start some employee program like a bowling league, or plan a company picnic. It's a way for management to say it cares about the employees. I really think this could affect morale and give the employees a spirit of wanting to work together—a cohesion they don't have.

Al and Fred: Good idea, Smitty!

Fred: I'd like to spearhead those activities, if it's OK with the group. I'm a bowling bug. Even though I'm no editor, it'd be interesting to find some reporters to dig up stories and put them together. I'm for it.

Phil: These are all worthwhile ideas. I appreciate your wanting to get things done. Fred, I'll be looking for your first publication. Al, the salary investigation is your department. And, Smitty, we'll leave the two gripers to you.

We've found some of the things that may be causing our problem of absenteeism. I appreciate your help in finding and resolving these situations. I'll be interested in getting feedback about your progress with your projects. Are there any other ideas we should go into about this or related matters?

OK. That's it for now, fellows.

EVALUATION

That's dialogue! The interaction speaks for itself. There's an obvious interchange of ideas between the parties involved. There's a desire on the part of all to share and participate. There's understanding, arrived at through verbalized feelings, attitudes, and ideas. All of the members employed a high degree of candor and freedom in their discussion. All were open in their evaluation of what might be the cause for the absenteeism.

In understanding Phil Dalton, the monologist, we see that his concept of conversation was to "tell" his people what *he* thought they should know. He was so preoccupied with himself that he lost touch with those to whom he was speaking. His concern was for himself and his view. Others exist to serve and confirm him; he wasn't really interested in the thinking of others. He presented his own interpretation or meaning as final and ultimate!

Carl Rogers observes in his book, *Client Centered Therapy*[1]:

"Individuals, from infants to old people, resent or fail to show any interest in anything initially presented to them through discipline, regulation or instruction which is another aspect of authority."

In the alternate approach, when we examine Phil, we find his dialogue exemplifies a more personal form of communication. It's more open, friendly, and warm—certainly more human. It permits a free flow of exchange of attitudes, feelings, and ideas. It seems to stimulate expressions of creative thinking by the group. One of its built-in advantages is that it allows Phil to express approval and recognition of his men.

Phil *reinforced* his men's acceptance and *raised* their self-esteem. These are two of the most important outcomes of dialogue. Dynamically, this helps to reduce the possibility of apathy and passivity on the part of the "team members." Phil realizes that by acknowledging to his men his approval of their performance, they'll be motivated to be more effective members of his team and leaders of their own.

CARDINAL RULE OF DIALOGUE

In this case we saw the cardinal rule of dialogue put to use repeatedly. The men attempted to *see and respond to the thoughts and feelings of each other.* They were mutually responsive. No one attempted to impose his will, as did Mr. Dalton. *Human relationships thrive on a balance of giving and taking and generally disintegrate when the flow is too much in one direction.* In this dialogue *they maintained a relationship because ALL parties wanted it.*

As this case illustrates, we must attempt to observe other people and respond to them and their needs. All of us are prone to becoming so involved in what *we* are saying, or listening to ourselves, or thinking of what *we* want to say next, that we fail to either see the other person's point of view or to respond to what he has said.

Dialogue is "speaking to and responding to" between persons, with meaning flowing between them despite misunderstandings. It's the interaction between people where there's give and take—not just of words, but of emotions and feelings with an *understanding of people and a resolution of problems as the goal.* This means that one doesn't impose his own view on the other, as Phil Dalton did. He presented his words as absolute truth, both irrevocable and definite. We should invite participation by all members of the group in an endeavor to understand other peoples' views, attitudes, and meanings.

People seek the climate to express themselves but, more importantly, they want approval from others, they want to be recognized, and they want to know that people care about them and what they think and feel. Through dialogue, people can feel in touch with each other. Mr. Dalton's "edict" had created an atmosphere of isolation because he permitted none of these needs to be met or expressed by anyone other than himself.

In essence, good conversation embodies understanding the other person, his feelings, his needs, his goals. From that point we can guide what we say to create an atmosphere of motivation for the other person, to stimulate his thinking, and to evoke cooperation and understanding in order to solve problems.

DIALOGUE, OUR PERSONAL MIRROR

Dialogue helps us to see ourselves, and our limitations. We live in a society confused by the mask of manners, platitudes, and superficial courtesies. *We attempt, because of this, to please everyone to the extent that we sometimes do not know who we really are!* Failing to see ourselves as others see us, it's difficult to continue with the pretext of adapting to everyone we meet.

The parable of the little chameleon illustrates this point graphically. There was once a small, very talented little chameleon. His owner was quite proud of him and constantly displayed his ability to change colors, depending on the color of the surface on which he was placed. The owner would put him on blue and he would turn blue; on green he would change his color to green; on something yellow, he immediately adapted his color to yellow. Even if he were placed on purple, he turned that color. Such a talented little chameleon! Such a proud owner!

Then one day, the owner met a lady wearing a plaid suit. He placed his little chameleon on the lady's plaid, and the poor chameleon blew apart!

Sometimes it would seem that because we attempt to adapt to people, this might be our end, too. Unless we're able to see our real selves and portray our real selves, that may well be our emotional fate. Fortunately, through conversation we can become aware of blind spots by listening to ourselves speak and listening to what we say, and "reading" the reactions we produce in others. Often we don't hear the facts as they really are until we say them aloud and get a reaction from another human being.

The things we verbalize may shock us since we have a tendency to hide ourselves from ourselves. Amazingly, we discover what we really are thinking and feeling when we verbalize to another. It's quite possible for us to find our own solutions to our problems through conversation and discussion with others *by listening to what we ourselves say.*

CAN DIALOGUE BE COMFORTABLE? SHOULD IT BE?

A tense situation aired in mutually honest dialogue results in a more comfortable feeling. To be meaningful, dialogue is a sincere, totally honest verbal exchange between two or more persons during which game-playing facades are dropped and the truth of each person is openly portrayed. Because of this, it's not always immediately easy and comfortable. Potentially, however, *the rewards are ease and comfort* with yourself and others. There's no way for this comfortable feeling to be achieved other than through honest, open dialogue. A tense situation won't just "go away." It may dim temporarily only to manifest itself at a later date and even in a different form. To relieve it, dialogue!

It's highly probable that there will be areas of nonunderstanding and disagreement as well as areas of agreement and understanding in healthy, vital dialogue. This is normal and it indicates that the people involved are "thinking people" who are willing to mention an area of dissent in order to have it understood. (The only time this would be unhealthy would be when the aim of the dialogue was to *intentionally* confuse or bring about disagreement, irritate, or cause misunderstanding.)

Human relationships can be healthy only where there is a balance of exchange, of give and take. A loss of interest or a loss of participation by either party can't be compensated for by stronger interest or participation on the part of the other. Each side must speak with openness. *A relationship is only as strong and vital as the weaker member.* The more even the balance of giving and taking, the stronger the relationship and the better the possibility to solve problems and resolve differences.

To deny or refuse participation is to reject a satisfying relationship, and unless a relationship is satisfying, it will not continue since at this point it is no longer comfortable.

Are there times when there is virtually no payoff or reward in attempting conversation? The following case indicates a loud and clear response to this question.

Case Study No. 2 / Forget It, Fella!

Tony, an account executive, has pursued a very important client, Harry Hollender, for several months now. Getting to him even by telephone was like trying to penetrate the walls of the Bastille. But Tony persisted and finally succeeded in making a luncheon appointment with H.H.

Intentionally, Tony was five minutes early for his appointment. As it turned out, he waited an additional twenty-five minutes for H.H. So, twenty-five minutes late for their reservation in a crowded restaurant, they had to wait for a table.

Hastily, H.H. suggested a martini at the bar to kill time. Tony didn't drink at noon, but he ordered tomato juice. H.H. quickly directed the bartender to make his martini a double.

H.H. and Tony exchanged remarks about the luncheon crowd and H.H. said, "Let's have another, bartender." Tony said, "Not for me." (He had hardly gotten past the Worcestershire sauce in his tomato juice.)

Tony asked H.H. what he thought about the local pro-football team, and the maitre d' signaled that their table was ready.

H.H. grabbed his double luncheon "appetizer," gulped it down with one slush, and said, "Bartender, a fast one to travel with!" Tony and tomato juice were still doing OK, so he again declined to reorder.

H.H. clutched his double and slithered to the table. (In case you aren't keeping score, that's two doubles (four singles) down and one double just delivered. *Total:* Six martinis in twenty-one minutes!)

OBSERVATION

Tony, forget H.H. He's already forgotten you. He's headed for his own never-never land. Better luck next time.

It's obviously a waste of time to attempt conversation with someone who's "in his own bag" because of alcohol.

Are there other instances where we might wonder what to do about "making conversation," whether to proceed or not to, and if so, how? The following illustration asks what you think you would do in a similar circumstance.

Case Study No. 3 / Hmmmmm, What to Do?

Arthur Wilson is senior vice-president of production of a sizable chemical firm in a metropolitan area. He has several thousand employees under his jurisdiction.

On this particular morning, as is his custom, he enters his office at 9:00 A.M. and proceeds to his desk. His secretary has opened all of his mail with the exception of one letter marked "Personal, Confidential." It bears a local postmark, and the plain white envelope has been addressed on a typewriter. Arthur opens it and reads:

"Sir: It is my duty as a citizen of this community to inform you that I am aware of some immoral transactions going on between two of your employees. I feel that you should know that your secretary, Rita Forbes, is having an affair with your assistant, Josh Grant. Before this gets to Mr. Grant's wife, I thought you should know about it.

"Yours truly,
A Concerned Citizen"

If you were Arthur, what would you do about this letter? It concerns your secretary, a single woman, and your assistant, a married man.

Some options include:

Discussing it with one or two people.
Disregarding the letter.
Sending it to the personnel department.
Referring it to the postmaster for investigation of misuse of the mails.

Arthur's reaction to this letter:

Arthur (musing to himself): This is a "crank letter." It could be just malicious gossip. Until I know our business is being affected by such a relationship, it's up to the two people involved how they handle their personal relationship outside of business hours. Their personal lives belong to them as long as their behavior doesn't interfere with their work or reflect on the company.

EVALUATION

This is one of those rare times when it would seem advisable not to engage in dialogue with either Josh or Rita. Morals are a touchy thing with which to deal. It's difficult to give credence to any anonymous letter. It might or might not be worth looking into. It could be a prank. Why stir up animosity by mentioning it?

People's personal lives are their personal property. There are times when it's better not to dialogue.

OMISSION CAUSES CONFUSION

Have you heard people say, "But that goes without saying"? Are there *ever* times when we can make this statement and expect it to be of value? It can be guaranteed that the most misunderstood statements in the world are those that have gone "without saying." Why? Because *people cannot read other peoples' minds!* (And if they could, they might read them incorrectly.)

It's imperative that we share our thinking with others. Sometimes we make assumptions that the other person will know what we mean, or what we want him to do, or what we expect of him in performance. *We should make fewer assumptions and make sure by expressing ourselves.*

Ben Jonson once said, "Speak so that I may know you." We must speak so that people are able to know us, to understand us. Literally nothing *goes without saying.* You can be sure that if it does, it may be totally misconstrued.

Moliere wrote, "It is not only what we do but also what we do not do for which we are accountable." We can paraphrase this to read, "It is not only what we say but also what we do not say for which we are accountable." It is still an error, by omission because we failed to express our thinking through verbalizing it.

Dialogue that is misunderstood, misspoken, and unspoken is the incubation point for confusion, for finding fault and for certain misunderstanding.

AN ANTIDOTE FOR ANXIETY

A certain amount of anxiety is good for us; like adrenaline, it propels us to action. In our country, there is an abundance of *un*healthy anxiety. Many man-hours are lost to illness resulting from the undue anxiety we experience daily.

Anxiety builds for us when we create it within ourselves by failing to effectively dialogue with others. Usually, the process will follow this pattern of formation:

1. We assume something to be a fact without knowing it to be so. We assume that something might (or might not) happen. We thus make a demand on ourselves.

2. By means of our imagination, we add catastrophe.

3. We say, mentally, "I can't take it if that happens to me. I'm sure it will!"

Anxiety is tiresome and wearing. It consumes much of our time and drains energy unnecessarily. Let's look at the case of Louis Mann to see how anxiety can build.

Case Study No. 4 / Case 1 Anxiety

Louis Mann is an accountant for a floor-wax company with several national outlets. One day, while attempting to work, he muses, "I know there's going to be a change made here—I can feel it in the air. I overheard them talking yesterday about someone 'having to go.'

"Wonder if they meant 'go' like getting the hatchet or 'go' like being transferred? That'd be the day! I can't afford to have either happen to me. I've been with this damned company for eleven years —they know I'm reliable, and I am—I'm a company man!

"What the hell would my family do—what would happen to them if I got transferred? The kids would have to change schools—that wouldn't work too well. We'd have to sell the crazy house and move —Ethel hates moving!

"She sure would be upset to uproot—she has lots of friends here, the PTA, the church club. Oh, and that damn bridge club of hers— she'd never leave that clan. She'd have to find all new friends. Ethel just wouldn't buy the idea of moving. I don't think I'm keen on it either! Now that I've said that—I wouldn't want to move; it would mean all new friends for me, too—no good!

"Worse yet would be to be fired! I'd end up looking for a new job. God, if there's one thing I hate, it's pounding pavements, and who knows for how long. Good jobs are hard to get. House payments, car payments, doctor bills, everything on credit—shit-impossible!

"Either way—to be fired or have to move—it'd be a crisis! It just can't happen! Damn, what'll I do if it *is* me they're thinking about changing?"

EVALUATION

Louis is really building a case of anxiety. Why?—One, he listened to rumor without clarification or verification; two, he made the assumption that he would be involved in a change that might be made; three, he produced catastrophe by envisioning all of the negative things that could happen; and four, he admitted to himself that he couldn't take it. This is the binding statement that triggers anxiety.

ALTERNATE APPROACH

Louis should try to find out what was meant by "someone going to have to go." He's being a solitary worrywart playing a game with his own negative thinking. You can create anxiety by yourself. You, singular, can do it all alone with the aid of your negative imagination. It's better to *talk it out*, to *find out what the accurate facts are.*

Individuals aren't born equipped to accommodate unnecessary anxiety, uncertainty, and tension. There can be less of all of these pressures when we engage in healthy dialogue to improve our understanding of ourselves and of others in order to solve our problems.

Dr. Paul Tournier says in *To Understand Each Other:*[2] "If the first condition for the achievement of understanding is the will to understand, the second condition is that of expressing oneself. Every human being needs to express himself. Through lack of opportunity for it, one may become sick."

Have you had a headache at work or because of your job? You aren't alone! You've got lots of company in this area. Many of these headaches are the result of the tension of business-related situations. Much of this tension is a direct result of keeping inside our head various feelings that we fail to verbalize. Tension builds to produce a headache, or backache, or ulcers, or, or, or. . . . If we would discuss what we're thinking, we could avoid much of the illness in today's society.

Dialogue can go a long way toward alleviating our inherent daily worries. It isn't a panacea, but it's more than a placebo. Thinking about a problem doesn't clear it up. In fact, we tend to magnify its seriousness when we keep it contained in our head. *Talk it out!* We may be surprised to discover that *it exists as a problem only in our thinking!*

DIALOGUE IN DECISION MAKING

How do most managers and businessmen spend the bulk of their day? What comprises your major activity during a business day? Usually decision making consumes most of your energy. In their book, *Critical Incidents in Management*,[3] Champion and Bridges state:

"The most characteristic task of the manager is decision making. The typical manager each day is confronted with decisions for which there are no precedents, no formulas, no procedural manuals, no established principles, and few, if any, factual premises."

Decisions of this type do drain energy, often unnecessarily. Most of our problems stem from this omnipresent responsibility. Our energy is burned up and wasted through indecisiveness!

Dialogue can help to minimize the period of indecision. It can also aid the manager in formulating procedures and resolving solutions.

There are people who seem to "always make the wrong decisions." Others of us make no decisions at all. Like weather vanes in a windstorm, we gyrate in circles until everything blends into a kaleidoscope of indecision and subsequent anxiety and frustration.

What about the man who seems to breeze through it all? He makes a decision and goes forward! How does he go about decision making? What's his pattern or procedure? He isolates the problem, discovers its causes, then seeks a solution. Now he's ready for action. Sound simple? It's easier if you're willing to dialogue. The manager uncovers "details" by talking with people about the problem and its causes. He obtains the thinking of others regarding possible solutions. Ultimately, the decision is made, solely by the manager, or in conjunction with group participation. Next, the plan is put into action.

To facilitate decision making, "talk it out." In this way we can better understand people with whom we have to relate, to get what's on their minds, to unleash their creativity. This makes working together easier, more comfortable, and more productive.

INVOLVEMENT vs. TELLING

Virile dialogue must be mutual; it must proceed from both sides. When it fails to do this, penalties result. We see negative attitudes developing en masse. There's apt to be a high degree of buck passing and office politics with little honesty and much superficiality.

When business is operated by the monologist, most of these symptoms are present. Why? Because he's *telling*. Adults and children alike just don't like to be told to do things! In resistance to being *told*, the co-workers often "clam up." They become passive, refusing conversation and participation.

In *Client Centered Therapy*,[4] Carl Rogers cites the following:

> A study by Coch and French comes to (this) conclusion regarding industrial workers. With conditions of pay held constant, some groups of workers were shifted to a new task and carefully instructed in the way to handle it and in ways of increasing efficiency on the new task. Other groups were shifted to the new task, and permitted to discuss, plan, and carry out their own way of handling the new problem. In the latter groups productivity increased more rapidly, increased to a higher level, held a higher level, and morale was definitely higher than in the groups which had been instructed.
>
> A study of supervision in an insurance company was made by the Survey Research Center. When units in which productivity and morale were high were compared with those in which they were low, significant differences were discovered in the methods and personalities of the supervisors. In the unit with high productivity, supervisors and group leaders tended to be interested primarily in the workers as people, and interest in production was secondary. Supervisors encouraged group participation and discussion and group decisions in matters affecting their work. Finally, supervisors in these "high" units gave little close supervision to the work being done, but tended to place the responsibility upon the worker.
>
> Other industrial studies, though less objective in nature, bear out the two that have been cited. Various industries, in this country and in Great Britain, have found that in quite divergent industrial situations there is improvement in effectiveness and in morale when workers are trusted as being capable of responsible handling of their own situation. This has meant a permissiveness toward their active participation in thinking about the issues, and a willingness for them to make, or participate in making, the responsible choices and decisions.

When two adults converse on an adult level, things can be accomplished. However, when one becomes the parent and the other the child, the relationship is potentially dangerous. When a manager says to an employee, "I'll *let* you make the decision," it's like the father saying to his son, "I'll grant you *my permission* to stay out until 9:30 P.M." Adult-to-adult says, "The decision is up to you," or "The decision is yours to make." The difference is the word "let." "Let" is permission giving and parentlike, and can evoke a negative mental response from the receiver such as "You'll *let* me make the decision! You and who else will *let* me?"

Isn't it more palatable for the receiver to get words as suggestions rather than as commands? If the sender says, "You can't do that!" or "You have to do that!", the reaction might be, "Says who? I'll do as I damned well please! I'll show you who's boss!"

The following incident exemplifies the difference between "tell" and "involve."

Case Study No. 5 / Just Busy Work

Harmon Beck is sales manager of some seventy-five men in a mid-south region. Since the men travel, all are involved with expense accounts. Harmon summons them for a Monday morning "discussion."

Harmon: This session has been called on Monday because you're going your separate directions for the rest of the week. I want to let you in on a bit of company policy. Due to the weakened economy, we've decided expense accounts have to be more detailed. They are not to be estimated but substantiated with receipts. They must be handed in every Monday morning. If all of these rules are not adhered to, you'll be charged 10 percent of your account for additional handling. Are there any questions about this? If not, you're dismissed. Have a good week!

PROBLEM

Authorative management! There was little room for, or encouragement of, dialogue. The salesmen might as well accept the new company edict.

ALTERNATE APPROACH

Harmon: Good morning, gentlemen. Before you begin another week "out there," there's something I'd like to discuss with you. Because of our economy drive, we need to review the matter of expense accounts. Any suggestions how we can cut back in this area?

Frank: I'll be honest with you, Harmon. In my book I think expense accounts are a lot of detail work. They take lots of time and energy and I don't enjoy that added paper work beyond my other reports.

Les: Lots of us consider them unnecessary detail work. We've discussed it! Maybe you'd like to know what we've considered?

Harmon: You bet I'm interested, Les.

Les: Well, to begin with, processing expense accounts costs a great deal. It takes time for the salesman, and for the bookkeeping department. It's busy work for all of us.

Some of us decided we'd be interested in getting a reasonable weekly allotment for our expenses. If we don't spend it all, we pocket the difference. If we spend over it, then that's tough for us. There might be a few things outstanding that we should be reimbursed for, but the room and board and mileage could be estimated from previous averages. How about giving us a flat figure for this and eliminate all the daily record keeping?

Frank: Good idea, Les. You're right, most of us know what our routine weekly expenses are. I'd sure be happy to get rid of submitting records on everything.

Harmon: That would eliminate the paper work here in the office, too. How do the others feel about this? Would you agree with this approach at least for a try? It would cut back detail work for you end expenses for us.

Group: Yeh!

Harmon: I'm glad to see you're willing to experiment with this on a trial basis. Let's see how it works for three weeks. We'll review it the following Monday and take it from there.

Thanks for your help and cooperation. Are there any other suggestions? Comments? Have a good week. It'll benefit all of us. Good luck!

EVALUATION

Harmon is exercising participative management. He allows possible solutions to grow from the group. In general, he has allowed dialogue rather than monologue to be the technique used to arrive at the group decision. He has found that through shared thinking, group participation, and group involvement, ideas that might otherwise remain undiscussed can be revealed.

SUPERIMPOSING OURSELVES

One of the pitfalls each of us as individuals faces daily is our wish to impose (superimpose) our attitudes and behavior on others.

We ask them to be as we are, to think as we think. We set ourselves up consciously or subconsciously as the *summum bonum*. We generously salt our dialogue with "Yes but——" We overlook the right of every other human being to be an individual, unique unto himself. We should remind ourselves of this fact during our conversations. When we do, we'll be better able to understand the needs of others, and to discover avenues for motivation.

The following incident is classic thinking "our way is the only way."

Case Study No. 6 / FloooooOOOOOM!

Cliff Tyson is a young real-estate salesman working in what has been a conservative section of the suburbs. The area is growing and has a new, young population. Cliff's previous sales record has been good, and his potential with this growth-neighborhood looks promising.

One morning, Cliff's manager, Sheldon, is seated at his desk when he hears a *FlooooooOOOOOOOM* noise at the parking area outside his window. He looks out to see Cliff parking a motorcycle. Helmet in hand, Cliff bounces into the office.

Sheldon: Good grief, Cliff, what are you trying to do, kill yourself?

Cliff: Heck no! How do you like it?

Sheldon: What? The motorcycle? You've gotta be kidding. I hate 'em!

Cliff: Sorry about that, Sheldon. That's my new wheels.

Sheldon: You're not planning to ride that damned deathtrap on calls, are you?

Cliff: Why not? It's great! Get with it, Sheldon. Everyone's doing it.

Sheldon: Yes, *but* not when you work here!

Cliff: Oh, come on now, Sheldon. Don't be so uptight about this.

Sheldon: I don't want you getting killed, Cliff. And besides, that's a hell of an image you'd make—representing this company on a motorcycle. I think it's stupid to even consider such a thing.

Cliff: Well, it may be stupid to *you*, but *I* think it's great.

Sheldon: You'd never catch me on a thing like that. It would destroy our image. I'd never live it down, having a salesman who rides a motorcycle. I just can't let you do it, Cliff.

Cliff: Well, hey now! If you can't *let* me do it, I don't think *I* want to do it any other way. Maybe we'd better forget the whole thing. I want to ride my motorcycle, and that's that.

Sheldon: Well, then, that *is* *that!* Your attitude isn't what I'd have expected from you, Cliff. It sounds as though we're at an impasse. You'd better just hop on your motorcycle and ride away.

Cliff: Good idea! I don't want to work for a straight boss like you anyway. I'll get my things.

PROBLEM

Sheldon has imposed his thinking on Cliff. He's asking—telling—Cliff that he must accept his values and make them his rules by which he, Cliff, will operate. Sheldon has failed to get Cliff's thinking or reaction as to why he's riding a motorcycle. He has *told* Cliff what he feels about the company image. There has been no exchange of values. The episode has been very one-sided on Sheldon's part. His attitude toward Cliff is parent-child with little consideration for what Cliff is feeling and why.

ALTERNATE APPROACH

Sheldon: Good morning, Cliff.

Cliff: It is a good morning, Sheldon. Did you see my new means of transportation?

Sheldon: First I heard it, then I saw it. And it *is* a motorcycle?

Cliff: That's right. The most "in" thing I could think of doing!

Sheldon: Cliff, Can you tell me why you want to ride a motorcycle?

Cliff: Well, I've figured it out this way. We live and work in a growing area. The folks who have lived here for years already have their property. They aren't really clients for me, anyway. It's the young, new blood that's coming out here who are buying the property. I think I can relate lots better to the younger set by riding a motorcycle.

Sheldon: Is what you're telling me that you're going to use it to call on prospects?

Cliff: Sure, why not? In my book, it's much more intelligent to be different and "with it." I can probably be the only real estate man in this area who rides a motorcycle, at least for awhile. That's as good as, or better than, driving a Rolls Royce, especially when my clients are the younger group. I feel we can identify better that way. It's a good icebreaker, and a pleasure for me at the same time, just as your Cadillac is a pleasure for you. We're both doing the same thing, only my "thing" costs lots less!

Sheldon: I hadn't thought of it that way, Cliff. My first reaction was to think you'd gone out of your mind! But it makes sense the way you say it. Let me put it this way. If it doesn't decrease your sales, I'll go along with you using it for business. How about proving the reverse, that it can actually *increase* your sales!

Cliff: Good challenge, Sheldon! It'd be my pleasure to do just that! Oh, by the way, I have an extra helmet. Would you like to go for a spin with me?

Sheldon: Get out of here! And make it pay off, you and your motorcycle, and I'll love you both!

EVALUATION

Sheldon has treated the situation on an adult-to-adult level. He sensed Cliff's keen exuberance over his acquisition. Sheldon respected Cliff's thinking. As long as it doesn't decrease sales, it's acceptable that Cliff rides his motorcycle for business.

Cliff kept the air pleasantly clear by leaving with a bit of humor.

Good management embodies getting the other person to "open up" so that each may better understand the other's point of view and problems. In refusing dialogue, we risk losing another's confidence, understanding, support, trust, and intelligence. Usually, in the process, we dehumanize ourselves. This is a high price to pay for not talking!

WHY DO PEOPLE REFUSE TO DIALOGUE?

One major reason why we refuse dialogue is because we fear; we fear a threat to ourselves, rejection by others, failure to meet another's expectations, hurt, disappointment, or being overruled. These are all the fantasies of *fear*. They are things we "fear" will happen if we dialogue.

We fear dialogue because we don't want to face facts or are afraid that someone will disagree with our thinking. If someone exposes another point of view, it could upset our plan and scheme of things.

Our greatest fear is exposing ourselves to another person. If we share ourselves, some weakness or prejudice might become known to the other. These fantasies are obstructions to communication. All have their stem, their root, in the word FEAR!

Employees are afraid to express their gripes about the company; it might be dangerous, or it might block a promotion for them. Their ideas may be used "without reward" or they'll be laughed at. Employees may even expect retaliation if they express their attitudes.

What then is fear? *Fear is concern about the unknown.* Once we recognize these obstructions, know how to handle them, and realize they are a part of conversation, we no longer have any need to fear.

As human beings, we tend to rationalize: "There really is no need for discussion" . . . "Management really doesn't want to hear from us" . . . "They really wouldn't understand." . . . What an uncomfortable life every day—to pretend, to keep things inside ourselves, to let this poison infect our bloodstream. Isn't it better to discuss things, talk things out, express ourselves for what we *really are?* How much less painful. How much more a real person we become.

Is it unusual for people to fear being open in conversation?—Not at all. Such obstructions to communication are part of each individual. It's as though certain genes produce this in all of us. There are no exceptions. Even people who are sophisticated in the art of conversation experience reservations and anxieties that prevent their speaking out, or that cause them to hear incorrectly—or to not hear at all.

Can we begin to overcome these fears as we recognize more of the fundamental dynamics of dialogue? Hopefully, but only when both sides are open with each other and attempt dialogue. Otherwise, faulty, strained relations will be the outcome. Lay aside the obstructions. Attempt open conversation.

Have you heard someone say, "My boss just doesn't understand me. Why should I bother trying to talk with him any further?" What this person is saying is, there's a barrier in their conversation. Unless this barrier is talked out, there can be little or no understanding. Resistance to understanding is part of dialogue. It must be accepted as such and not feared, but faced and erased.

Dialogue demands that there be a flow of conversation between both sides. This flow must be mutually sustained if problems are to be solved. *We must attempt to stand in the other person's shoes, to understand his thinking, to understand what he is trying to get across. We should strive to keep an open mind to the other person's point of view and to discover why it is as it is.*

Case Study No. 7 will indicate the need to uncover the real meaning of what a person is saying.

Case Study No. 7 / Hold It, Clarence!

Travis Nelson and Matt Frazier are sitting in the outer office of T. Clarence Sutton, their president, when he strides by them with a brusque, "I want to see the two of you!" Both look at each other, then silently follow Clarence into his office and close the door behind them.

Clarence: All right, the two of you! What's going on with that contract you were supposed to have submitted three weeks ago to the Delaware Press?

I just found out it hasn't been returned. Why wasn't I told about it? You never follow through with anything you're supposed to. You're always goofing around about something else when I need to talk to you. Why don't I get some quick reactions from you about important matters?

Never mind, never mind. I don't want to hear any excuses from you. You'd better get on the ball about that Delaware contract and track it down or we're sure to lose the account.

Well, don't just stand there. Get moving!

(Exit Travis and Matt.)

PROBLEM

An authoritarian manager who deals in parental telling, absolutes, no listening, and commands and demands.

POSSIBLE SOLUTION

Clarence: Matt, Travis, be seated!
Travis: I get the feeling that there's something *wrong!*
Matt: Let's have it, Clarence. What is it?
Clarence: The Delaware Press contract. What the hell's happened with it? It should have been sent out three weeks ago.
Matt: It was sent out but it isn't back.

Travis: Hold it, Clarence. You're making assumptions about something you haven't asked about. No use getting that high blood pressure of yours higher when it isn't necessary. I checked that contract about ten days ago when it hadn't come back. The guy who was supposed to sign it has been on vacation and will be for about another week.

Matt: We weren't sitting on it. We did check it out and, for that matter, we were assured he'd attend to it first thing when he gets back.

Travis: I appreciate your concern about this, Clarence, but I wish you could trust us enough to know that we're not asleep on the job.

Clarence: I know that. I do trust you, both of you.

I had a little interruption coming down today. For some stupid reason I got a citation on the expressway that's going to set me back fifty bucks—totally uncalled for, of course.

Besides it costing me money, that little stop made me late getting here. The first thing I heard when I walked in was that the Delaware Press contract hadn't come back. Then when I saw you two——.

It helps to have you to take the blow. Sorry I exploded at you like that. It really was a combination of things that hit the steam valve and made it go off. I'm glad to know you're on top of the contract. Let me hear from you as soon as it's returned—*signed!*

Travis: I've gotten a few tickets in my time. It's a good thing you weren't around then or *I'd* probably have blasted *you!*

Matt: Call if there's another bomb that needs detonating.

Clarence: Get out of here, you two. And thanks.

EVALUATION

A sense of humor throughout saved what might have been an ugly scene. There's a feeling of friendship and trust even with the gravity of Clarence's attitude.

Clarence shared his citation incident and, by verbalizing, relieved much of his tension. Sharing this episode pinpoints the fact that the contract incident was not the initial cause for Clarence's consternation. He focused on the real problems—getting the ticket and being late.

The tense scene ends with the air cleared and with a sense of humor being exhibited in the spirit of good friendship and under-standing.

There may be merit in another's thinking, and we can benefit by this thinking only if we allow it to be expressed. Clarence's anxiety was relieved when he learned the things that Travis and Matt knew. Considerable concern can be saved when the other person divulges facts in his possession. Clarence could have saved his high blood pressure by asking Travis and Matt about the contract. Instead, he built his anxiety by making assumptions. *Is it possible to work effectively when working with assumptions? It is much easier to work effectively when one is in possession of factual information.* Clarence couldn't deal effectively with this situation of the unsigned contract without further confirmation and facts from Travis and Matt. Yet, in the heat of his anxiety, he attempted to do just that. Had he proceeded without talking with Matt and Travis, he could have created an awkward situation. It appeared to be more comfortable for all when Clarence stated why he was tense and upset! *Clear the air with facts.*

FORMS OF DIALOGUE

Trivia

Does all dialogue have to be so serious? Talking is a compulsion in our American society. We meet through minds rather than meeting through feelings. We've been brought up on superficial politeness and palaver—trivia, some call it.

When we first meet, the quality of our words is of less relevance than the quantity. Trivia is a usual thing on the social level.

When meeting socially, we engage in "cocktail-party talk," on subjects both parties usually couldn't care less about. This type of dialogue *can* be a bore!

Are there times when trivia has a place and worth? Yes, indeed! Trivia is a way of breaking the ice, a way to say hello. Animals smell each other to get acquainted. Islanders look (stare) to evaluate each other. Americans talk. In this way, we have a chance to size up other people.

Trivia is a great wedge to use in easing tensions. When the air is "heavy," trivia can sometimes lighten it. When tension manifests itself in the form of silence, trivia can break the silence and, hopefully, lead to meaningful discussion of the cause of the tension.

Trivia also allows for relaxation in dialogue. It feels good to be relieved for awhile of mental gymnastics and verbal intellectualization. Sometimes, it's *good* to just "trivia"!

Gossip

Gossip is another form of conversation, a "cousin" to trivia. It, too, is a form of dialogue. Gossip exists at every level of society. It may take the form of an escape valve, which the following instance exemplifies.

Case Study No. 8 / Can You Top This?

Ross and Albert work for the same company. They have different superiors to whom they report in different departments. They're casual friends and happened to meet during coffee break.

Ross: My boss sure doesn't understand me!

Albert: Your boss doesn't understand you? You should work for the guy I report to!

Ross: He couldn't be as bad as my boss. Why, he never has time to talk about anything.

Albert: That's nothing. I've only seen my boss once in the last six months. I only get memos when I've done something wrong.

Ross: Well, I'm lucky to even get a memo. Usually this guy's secretary tells me off.

Albert: I'll tell you, I'd rather it'd be a secretary. At least it'd be a human being. A memo's pretty cold.

Ross: He should come around once in awhile, just to see if I'm still alive. I could have sent in a substitute and he'd never know it.

Etc., ad infinitum!

PROBLEM

Ross and Albert are playing "Can you top this?" So, what's wrong with playing this once in awhile? There's no big earthshaking problem to be solved. If these men get some of their steam off with this kind of meaningless gripe, why not let them have it?

EVALUATION

There is a problem here that lies between each of the men and their respective bosses. Each man should level with his boss and tell *him* how he feels.

This is an innocuous form of gossip. It serves the same purpose as trivia, to simply make conversation. Gossip can be a harmless exchange of insignificant thoughts, or the reverse can be true. Gossip can be damaging. When it's of that nature, it should be labeled BEWARE! It should be evaluated and handled as dangerous and explosive! When such information is passed along, it may be damaging to a situation or to a person. If confidential material is discussed, it could be disastrous. As it's transmitted from one person to another, gossip can lose what truth was contained in its original verbalization. When it becomes distorted, it can be dangerous.

The Grapevine

What about the grapevine? It's an extension of trivia and gossip. In business, the grapevine is one channel through which trivia and gossip are transmitted.

To a manager this can be a meaningful source of information. A grapevine can be valuable in registering a pulse on the thinking and attitudes of workers. It often reveals things the employees might not say to a manager on a one-to-one basis.

Some advice on using the grapevine is given by R. W. Planck's in the January, 1971, issue of *Modern Office Procedures*[5]

Clever managers often get things done simply by planting information in the office grapevine. But if you elect to use this informal line of communication, there are some guidelines to keep in mind: 1. Never try to use the grapevine maliciously. Remember—no trust, no communication. And you *could* lose your credibility along formal lines of communications: 2. Don't use the grapevine unless you can't get the job done via standard management techniques. Make sure you understand the situation, the people, and what can happen if your attempt fails: 3. Don't let the grapevine run you. Be sure that subordinates don't use the grapevine to sucker you into their way of thinking: 4. Find out who the talkers are and how the news travels. There may be more than one channel of communication: 5. If you're a middle-manager, be aware of the grapevine above you. Top management grapevines are dangerous and complex: 6. Don't boast about success at grapevine management. Superiors may think that you're devious and subordinates will distrust you.

Should you put the office grapevine to work? The answer is a qualified yes.

Silence

"Be still and know." Silence itself is a form of conversation. Pauses in dialogue can be valuable as "recappers" and "recoupers." This interim of no verbalization gives us time for our mental processes to recap what has been said. It also gives us time to recoup from the verbal and mental gymnastics of a deep or involved exchange of dialogue. It's good battery-recharging time; it should be enjoyed. Then we're able to resume, refreshed and reactivated to engage again in interpersonal communications. This is healthy silence.

Unhealthy, though, is lethal silence. This is strained, dead-air silence, the kind that kills emotions. It denotes tension and a possible impasse. It can be the most lonely feeling in the world to sit in tense silence *with someone else.* It can be a feeling of isolation, punishment, rejection.

When felt as such, it indicates the existence of a parent-child relationship. It's the parent punishing the child by putting him in the corner to sit in silence. It's the parent shaming the child by not including him in conversation or activities. It's the parent isolating the child, sending him to his mental-room to think things over.

How can we break this unhealthy silence? Sometimes a simple statement can do it—"Your silence tells me something, but I can't read your mind," or "I hear lots of feelings going on in this silence. Can you tell me what you're feeling right now?"

These are examples of simple sentences that can serve as wedges to break the silence. If such statements (or similar ones) don't bring forth conversation, bail out! This sort of tension is cruel and inhuman. It's nonproductive. Usually nothing constructive comes from it. It builds additional hostility, frustration and resentment. If it can't be broken with some ease, take a walk! It's better to walk out and come back to it at some later appointed time. It's unnecessary that we subject ourselves to such parent-child treatment. As mature adults we have gained the healthy right to be treated as mature adults!

There are other times when silence can be appropriate. When sympathy is needed, the best quality is often silence. It demonstrates respect, and surely, there is no advice to be given where there is grief. When someone is bereaved, it's unwise to attempt arguing them out of it or kidding them out of it. Equally as unsympathetic is over-sympathy! Just be quiet.

Silence may be appropriate when a person is hostile. At that moment it's hardly profitable to play amature psychiatrist in an attempt to figure out why, or to engage in giving advice. Just try silence while the boiler lets off steam. Your silence can be the best immediate help a hostile person can receive.

Then, there's your *own* silence when you're alone with YOU. This can be a blessing. It's healthy for us to get away from everyone and everything, to be alone. There are five divisions of time alone that are vital to you, the manager. Time to be—

> alone on the job,
> alone with your mate,
> alone with your children,
> alone with yourself,
> alone with your God.

COUNSELING WITH DIALOGUE

Counseling is a major tool of the manager to help him to discover his employees. What about written testing, performance check lists, review forms, standard of performance, rating lists, etc? Each is good in its place. But its place is usually a filing cabinet since they're used much too infrequently. Through verbal counseling, the manager can better know and help to evaluate the performance of his subordinates. In this way, subordinates can better learn what management expects of them; they gain insights into their performance, their strengths, and weaknesses. Counseling must involve dialogue— seeking out problems, discovering causes, attempting to resolve a course of action for improvement. And the payoff?—By implementing this technique, ideas are shared, growth encouraged, frustrations minimized, and goals established. Progress is made.

The manager's job is easier when he has the cooperation of those above and below him. As the middle man he is more apt to achieve his goals through upper management and his subordinates when he has healthy relationships. Through dialogue he can accomplish this upward and downward cooperation. As Emerson said, "Speech is power to persuade, to convert, to compel."

When a manager involves in effective interpersonal communications he has three immediate payoffs. He is able to:

1. Define needs, locate problems, and seek solutions.

2. Focus on an employee's strengths rather than on his weaknesses.

3. Gain closer contact with people, directing their creativity and in turn allowing them to stimulate his imagination.

These factors will help engender a spirit of teamwork. When you have employees working together effectively you have:

Improved the climate for productivity.
Decreased the possibility of turnover.
Set the stage for increased profits.

HOW CAN WE MOTIVATE PEOPLE?

When motivational needs aren't met, dialogue can disintegrate into silence. For verbal communications to be effective, it's essential that we understand how the motivation of people develops.

As Dr. Alfred J. Morrow comments in *Behind the Executive Mask*.[6]

However completely mechanized and automated our economy may be, it remains more than ever management's task to learn how to get the best out of people. This means that management must understand the motives of people, must study what effect organizational policies have on the mature individual, and must know how best to communicate with him. The productivity and profits of a business follow from the teamwork of its personnel, from the management of men— not from handling machines.

An individual is motivated by an atmosphere in which he's stimulated to motivate himself. *Motivation has to come from within the individual. The manager must strive to create a climate in which an individual motivates himself to perform in a particular manner.* The choice is his whether he chooses to act, or not to act, on the stimuli we have prepared for him.

James Cash Penney said that executive success ". . . is getting things done through other people. One must develop the art of getting people to do what you want them to do because they themselves want to do it."

When a sales manager dreams up a glorious holiday bonus for reaching a specific sales quota, it doesn't mean all of his men will be stimulated to produce enough to win the holiday. Some salesmen might produce just as much if the reward were to have their names mentioned weekly in the regional office bulletin. Management fulfills different needs in different ways.

How do we recognize these needs? Elementary knowledge of the five general areas of human needs will give us our foundation. Then, through dialogue we discover which of these needs exist in various individuals. Frequent one-to-one conversations give us the necessary insight to know a person better.

To become familiar with the general areas of human needs, let's turn to the genius of the late Dr. Abraham Maslow, who set forth these guidelines for us in his book, *Motivation and Personality.*[7] Individual needs break down into five categories:

1. Physiological (I need food, drink, clothing, and shelter).

2. Safety (I want security (financial) and protection (physical)).

3. Belongingness (I need love, affection, and identity).

4. Esteem (I want to like myself. I want others to like me).

5. Self-actualization (There's so much I'm sure I'm capable of which I haven't accomplished. Lord, show me the way). (See Figure 1.)

Although these needs appear in sequence, they don't always occur that way. Frequently, they may be interrelated, with more than one existing simultaneously. Generally, they occur in somewhat this order. As one is displaced, it's replaced by another.

A man may be a struggling, impoverished artist. He has needs that are more important to him than money, food, and shelter—his needs are for self-actualization. As long as he can get "a crust of bread," his great need is to display his talent, to be recognized for his abilities. He's gone out of the usual sequence of needs.

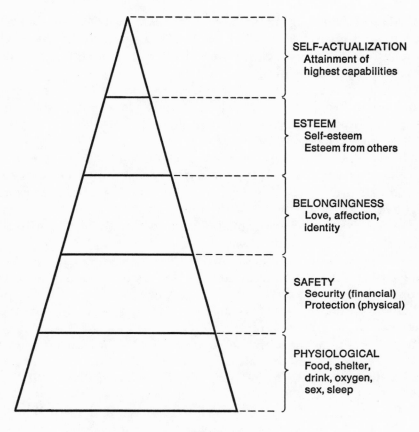

FIGURE 1

Let's go back to the sales contest. Most of the men who qualify for the holiday trip will be the ones who already have good incomes and could afford the trip out of their own pocket. Why then would the contest be so important to them? It satisfies their ego or self-esteem need. Winning the trip gives them recognition; it says, "I'm a big producer! I produced enough to get to go on the trip."

To examine these forces further:

1. *Physiological needs* are by far the most basic. These embody man's great need for self-preservation. He must have food, drink, shelter, sex, and oxygen. If a person is lacking in oxygen, water, and sex, his first demand will be for oxygen, the second for water, then sex.

As has been proven in prisoner-of-war camps, the sex drive may diminish to zero as a result of improper amounts of food and liquid. Men and women living in the same area seemingly had no sex drive because their needs for food and water were not satisfied. Until our very basic needs are met, we tend to ignore all others in a drive to satisfy them. But, as Maslow said, man is a craving, wanting being, and as soon as one need is satisfied, he's desirous of something else.

2. *Safety needs*, in the realm of business, mean security—security in the form of pension plans, Social Security, unemployment compensation, job security, etc. Currently there is another safety area that is entering our scene, safety from harm. We're becoming increasingly concerned with crime and the rampant rage of the drug scene. We're looking for protection and safety from these influences. In addition, there is mounting concern over safety for the entire human race because of pollution. Ecology is an important new safety need that industry must consider.

Why is industry concerned about this? Many younger people coming into the business world are less interested in a high salary and more interested in having a day off where they can be involved in ecological activities for the community. In addition, they don't want to associate with products and companies that do not adhere to standards for an improved ecology.

3. *Belongingness needs* usually come into focus when physiological and safety needs are met. There then emerges a need for love, affection, and belongingness. The individual now attempts to find a group with whom he can identify. Usually he relates to his peers and seeks to find acceptance within that group. In business the clubs, teams, award groups, cliques, and so on will satisfy these needs.

In addition, his need for personal love is strong and urgent, not just physical love (sex) but the deep love of belongingness that stems from sustained relations with someone of the peer group. The personal life of the individual is quite relevant to his job success. Dr. Maslow felt that the absence of love stifles growth and the development of potential.

4. *Esteem*. What is it? It's respecting ourselves and having others respect us. It's possible to like ourselves better when someone else likes us first, yet we have to like ourselves before others will like us. The esteem of self and the esteem we get from others seem to be inseparable. Which happens first? Seemingly they happen simultaneously.

Self-esteem means, "I have self-confidence. I think I can be somebody. I know I can do it! I'm independent. I *can* achieve." Esteem from others says, "You're a great guy. I like you. You did a great job. You're our number-one producer. You're important to the team."

These are vital factors in motivation for the manager. They're the attention and recognition sparkplugs that start most motors and the oil that keeps the motors running smoothly. Where these needs aren't satisfied, there's a feeling of rejection, unworthiness, and dejection. Deflated egos mean deflated production and deflated profits. *Remembering to inflate egos is of prime importance to the manager.*

5. *Self-actualization needs* are usually the last to be sought and attained. This isn't always true, but we tend to stay in need areas of belongingness and esteem for a long time. Frequently, we never rise above looking for more than that. When we do, we're looking to achieve our fullest potential. This often involves creativity.

Although creativity is usually associated with things aesthetic, let's define it here as meaning, finding a better way to do things. This involves art, perhaps. Yet, in the world of industry and business it can mean raising a corporation's production and profit statement to read an increase of 3 percent on its return on investment capital. It might mean attempting to guide and direct your organization to open new branches or plant sites. It could involve your efforts to bring to fruition franchising for your company or a merger, etc. The combinations are endless in business, where there's a tremendous need for people to desire self-actualization. Usually this desire becomes most active when we have satisfied other needs.

Additional need areas for workers

In *The Motivation to Work*,[8] Dr. Fredrick Herzberg indicates that there are some factors within the work situation that are sources for dissatisfaction, while others are primarily sources of positive motivation. He classifies factors that can produce irritation if not satisfied as hygiene factors:

1. *Physical*—Employees have certain requirements for their physical well-being that must be met: conditions of on-the-job-safety, clean and adequate rest rooms, parking space, temperature control, ventilation, eating facilities, etc.

2. *Social*—Employees need to interrelate with their associates: sports events, parties, clubs, lunch, coffee breaks, etc.

3. *Status*—Employees require identities with their organization that establish their roles within the company: job title, job description, badges, job privileges that go with the position, etc.

4. *Orientation*—The employees must know how they fit within the function of an organization, what their relationship is with the activities around them: rules, newspapers, bulletin boards, shop talk, memos, etc.

5. *Security*—A vital area of importance to employees is that of job security: seniority rights, friendliness, fairness of treatment, etc.

6. *Economic*—well-being is of prime importance: wages and salaries, benefits, commissions, bonuses, etc.

The primary result of the satisfaction of these needs is to alleviate dissatisfaction and its consequences. Their satisfaction does not necessarily mean motivation, but if they aren't satisfied they can cause lots of static.

We can work more effectively with people when we understand the level of their needs. Through efficient dialogue we can focus on these needs; through efficient dialogue we can aid employees to satisfy these needs through their job.

As Robert Townsend says in *Up the Organization:*[9]

Get to know your people. What they do well, what they enjoy doing, what their weaknesses and strengths are, and what they want and need to get from their job.

Through dialogue, we discover needs. When we find a man who is trying to buy a home, we know money will be a motivator for him. When dialogue reveals a socially conscious individual, the prestige of title and rank may be his motivator. Someone else has a great desire to be a member of a group. Being a part of a work team will help satisfy his needs.

What about the person who seemingly has everything? He may be in the area of self-actualization. When dialogue discloses this, it may also reveal that his need is to feel his business challenges him to build a better organization, or that he's making a contribution to ecology or some social cause. This will satisfy his self-actualization needs. We can uncover these specific areas through dialogue.

In all of us is the need for self-esteem. One of the greatest ways to gratify this is through business—work. A job well done is great reward in itself. In addition, when we receive verbal praise for the job well done, our self-esteem hits the 100-percent mark! *Human needs can be recognized and satisfied through good business management.*

Energizers
of
Dialogue

LEARN TO LEVEL

Payoffs for leveling

"There's nothing so powerful as truth and often nothing so strong." So wrote Webster. And isn't it the truth! To be honest, to level, to be frank and sincere can activate other people in highly positive ways. What's the payoff here and now for the manager in leveling?

He establishes trust since he tells the truth.
He builds confidence because he can be trusted.
He develops rapport from his openness.
He anticipates tensions and doesn't let them build.
He shares with others so they know exactly where he stands.
He manages with truth, and truth is easier to live with.
He gains respect through his sincerity.

It seems that management is an area where people won't buy facade, at least not for long. It's possible to fool others for a short time but the truth will out! To win respect and trust and appreciation, we must level and be honest. We can't communicate with someone we can't respect.

We manipulate people when we fail to level with them. We aren't honest, we don't share, we say what we think will be to our advantage and yield results that *we* want, disregarding the feelings and needs of others involved. Figures 2 and 3 illustrate the effects of leveling vs. manipulating.

In our society, we have to *learn* to level. Why?—Because leveling is socially learned behavior. In the past our culture, our society, and our educational patterns didn't emphasize either leveling or dialogue. Often the approach was not to oppose anyone in authority. As children our authoritarian upbringing said: "Don't talk back to your parents" .. "Be quiet" . . . "Leave well enough alone" . . .

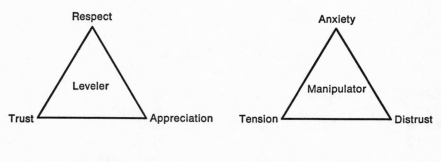

FIGURE 2   **FIGURE 3**

"Mind your own business" . . . "That's enough out of you!" These bromides of childhood gave us early training not to level. Our educational process equipped us in a similar manner: Listen to what your teachers say; don't question or doubt them. Just inhale their breath and that's what's right. Even if they have halitosis, just inhale! Management stressed "follow the leader"—ideas come from him, decisions come from him, direction comes from him. The leader is the leader! So we grew to be a group of less-than-levelers. This doesn't necessarily imply we're a "bunch-o'-liars"!

There are two types of not leveling: one, a commission—being untruthful; the other, an *omission—not sharing facts and ideas. Most of us fall into the latter category. We omit leveling. It's such an everyday occurence we sometimes don't recognize it.*

What then is the goal of leveling? The goal of leveling should be to change our whole management attitude and approach from one of win-lose to one in which both win. Leveling is an essential step in the process aimed at taking dialogue away from being a manipulative contest in which there must be one winner—one loser, and makes it instead effective dialogue with both parties sharing in the results. Not always 100-100, but 80-20, 60-40, 30-70, with both parties reaping some of the benefits for their input.

Leveling can be a sign of managerial maturity. It tells the other person that you can "tell it like it is" and not feel he'll dislike you; that you can deal in problems, not personalities; that you're mature enough to deal openly and objectively rather than subjectively. Through your candor, you tell him, "I'm an adult and I respect you as an intelligent adult. I feel I can level with you." It adds to self-confidence for both sides. Leveling can develop long-term friendships of trust and respect. One major payoff is you will always feel more comfortable with a person with whom you can level. After all, you don't have to remember what fabrications you told him before!

When truth is withheld, the effects are bound to be negative. The results are inevitably distrust and can lead to cynicism, suspicion, scorn, and treachery. It's impossible to encourage belief in an individual (and/or company) when truth isn't at the basis of the relationship. Cervantes put it this way: "Truth will rise above falsehood as oil above water."

Jefferson's *Theory of Democracy* develops the premise that full knowledge leads to right action and that right action is impossible without full knowledge. The manager and the management process can be more successful in possession of what effective facts it can possibly obtain from all its workers. One way this is feasible is through leveling in dialogue. Unexpressed ideas and creative thinking are omissions of knowledge that impede the progress and growth of an organization.

Pitfalls in not leveling

Pitfalls are inevitable when people won't level. They're the result of people who *omit* saying something important, or who don't tell the truth. In either instance, they can cause disastrous results.

1. *Sandbagging:* A gripe not aired becomes a grudge; then someone is apt to get sandbagged. The following story makes this point:

Dan Franklin, the president, and Bud Brown, his manager, were the two officers working in the office of a lumber company of some twenty-five employees. They reported to a board of directors quarterly. The balance of the office workers were women who reported to either Dan or Bud. It was a family arrangement with Dan and Bud splitting duties.

It became obvious that Dan was away from business frequently. The fact became known he was moonlighting during daylight hours. Essentially he was taking lumber, using it in his side business as a contractor, and failing to report it on inventories. Most of the office was somewhat aware of this, Bud was keenly aware of it since he handled the inventories. In addition, when Dan wasn't there, Bud had to assume his work load. However, Bud said nothing. He just kept working harder, and burning hotter, about the whole situation.

Dan would breeze in for an hour or two daily. Frequently he found fault with some of the women in front of other workers, and sometimes in front of customers. This, too, irritated Bud. He liked the office crew and didn't relish seeing them treated this way. However, no one ever confronted Dan about these things. Finally, one day Dan blew up at Bud behind closed doors. No one knew what was said, but they heard loud words from Dan.

From that day on, Bud began collecting evidence of things Dan was doing that weren't just according to Hoyle. He carefully notated and dated customer complaints about Dan. Dates of scoldings of office help were notated. Copies were kept of invoices that weren't "just right," etc. All were secured in the locked bottom drawer of Bud's desk.

Then, two years later, there was a board meeting. Bud intentionally walked in five minutes late. All were assembled, including Dan. Bud began the meeting. "Gentlemen!" he said. And with that he produced all the evidence against Dan that he had collected in the last two years. He even taped some of the encounters that took place in the office between Dan and salesmen. The most damaging evidence was the invoice copies showing Dan had literally embezzled many thousands of dollars of lumber to use in his construction business. *Bud sandbagged Dan!*

The little lumber company now has a new president, and a new manager. Both were replaced because of this incident. It was obvious why Dan was replaced, but why was Bud replaced? The board was furious that he had been in possession of all this information for all this time and hadn't imparted it to them. They considered him an unfaithful employee as much as Dan. He had failed to level with them about all these incidents that were costing the company money and losing profits.

Perhaps the sandbagging wouldn't have happened if, from the inception of their relationship, Dan and Bud had been able to level with each other. Then it might have been a possible working situation. As it was, it deteriorated to spite, hate, and sandbagging, which in turn cost both of them their jobs. It's better to air gripes as they happen. If they aren't aired, they become grudges.

2. *Thinking for two:* As human beings we have a tendency to speak for other people when we really don't know "where they're at." We'll say, "I know you wouldn't be happy in that territory. It would

necessitate a move for you and your family, so I've assigned Jay to that area." Why not *ask* and refrain from doing another's thinking for him? *We can't be responsible for anyone but ourselves.* It's selfish to think we're so important that we take on ourselves the responsibility of making decisions for someone else. *Only they can make their decisions.* We really can't make either the decision or the choice for someone else. If we do, it's sure to cause conflict. We can reach a decision mutually, through dialogue, but if it involves a decision to be made by another, let him make it for himself.

3. *Making assumptions for others:* There are many managerial varieties of this category. Making assumptions includes assuming an employee is capable of running a certain machine. You fail to explain how it's operated since you *assume* he knows how. Later, as you walk by the machine you see the employee just fiddling with it. You ask him what he's doing. He tells you he's trying to figure out how to operate this machine. Then you know you've made an assumption for the person when you should have asked for verification.

This is an incident in assumptive behavior:

In a large company John Rogers was brought in to head several departments, among them communications. John had been preceded by an authoritarian manager who gave specific directions down to the last detail, who ruled the creative group with restrictive paternal guidance, who was the decision maker, and so on. John was the exact opposite of his predecessor. He felt his people should be allowed a directed but free reign in expressing their creativity. He reorganized the department, giving certain people certain responsibilities and allowing them to be responsible for their decisions—to really participate.

One day, John called an editor into his office and they discussed at length a new project. The editor was enthused and eager to get involved in the work. John assessed this task would take about four working days for completion, five at the most.

Two weeks later, John hadn't heard from the editor regarding the project. Finally, he called him about it. The editor's reply was, "I was waiting for you to ask for it, Mr. Rogers. It's been completed almost ten days now."

It was all John could do not to berate the editor for this stupidity. After he had calmed down, he asked that the project be brought to him for review. Meanwhile, he had to admit to himself that he *had made the assumption* the editor would notify him when his work was completed. He failed to consider the fact this editor had recently worked under a man who would never have approved such presumption on the part of a worker. The former manager would have either specified a time for the editor to bring the work to him, or he'd have called to find out about it. John made an assumption that the editor would come to him. He paid the price for having made this assumption.

Specify, specify! There are times when guidelines and parameters are needed.

4. *Hitting "below the belt"*: When we don't drain off temper and anger through leveling, it's bound to create a buildup that eventually has to explode. At times such as these, we're apt to strike and hit below the belt. Irritations can accumulate to crest in a frenzy that's uncontrollable when it lets go. When this happens and we're really out of control of our leveling devices, we don't hear ourselves or anyone else. The following happening demonstrates this premise.

This incident concerned Joe Pence, who was foreman in a printing shop. He had seven men working under him. Among them was a burly man named Fran Roberts. Fran had been hired by the big boss about a year ago. He'd been a steady worker, quiet and reliable. He took lots of ribbing about his burliness and having the name Fran. He accepted this with a brief smile and worked on.

For no apparent reason, Joe had been at odds with Fran the past few weeks. He'd ask Fran to do extra things, put heavier work loads on him, more than his share. He needled him about irrelevancies. He was constantly "on Fran's back" about something.

The other men in the shop sensed the growing antagonism between the two. One day, the inevitable happened. Joe addressed the group with, "Look, Frannie's cut his little finger, poor little Frannie!"

The whole group laughed. Fran turned and in a white heat of anger said "Stop bugging me, man!"

Joe railed back, "You try to make me stop, you dirty ex-con!" With this, the fight was on. Finally the other six men pulled them apart.

Subsequently it was suggested to Fran that he "might want to leave." He did.

What had Joe done? He had hit Fran below the belt when he called him an ex-con. What caused all of this to happen? Joe had discovered Fran's previous prison record. When he did, he failed to mention it to anyone. When he started his needling, Fran guessed that Joe knew about his past, but he didn't open up to talk it out with him. Finally, as a result of neither man leveling, Joe hit Fran below the belt, the fight ensued, and Fran was out of his job.

Joe should have accepted Fran for his year's performance record. His previous record shouldn't have entered into the picture. Question No. 5 on a standard application blank asks if you've ever been arrested. Fran's employer knew of his record but agreed to employ him. Therefore, any discussion of this should have been between Joe and the employer who hired Fran.

An evaluation of this case with Mel Rivers of the Fortune Society, a national organization for penal reform, suggested that Fran should have been judged on his performance record only. Mr. Rivers felt Joe's only responsibility was to see that Fran did his job, not to delve into his past history. Background shouldn't change a man's productivity. That he worked effectively for a year was the important thing. Mr. Rivers admits that when there's a personality clash between someone who's been in prison and a superior, the former is sitting on a time bomb, as in the case of Joe and Fran. Again, Mr. Rivers reinforces this premise that a person should be judged on his achievement, not on his past history. "If I've been doing a good job, I only change when you change," says Mr. Rivers. "It's that way with anyone. Why should it be any different just because someone has served time?"

5. *Trap setting:* Trap setting is the neat little device we spring on people because we've failed to level about what we expect of them. They spring the trap when they fail to meet our expectations to perform as we feel they should (or shouldn't). Case in point:

Case Study No. 9 / "Key? What Key?"

Allen has recently located in the home office of a large corporation. He's spent many years at the local and regional level, so this is a new ball park to him. But he's quite competent, dapper and glib, and seems to take things in his stride.

After some two weeks in his new environment, Allen's called into his boss's office. Mr. Frost greets him with this chilly conversation.

Mr. Frost: Come in, Allen. There's something I want to discuss with you.

Allen: I'll give you odds whatever it is, it's old Allen's fault!

Mr. Frost: I'm afraid you're right, Allen. Several of the other executives have brought it to my attention that you've been riding the elevators with the other employees.

Allen: Well, yes! I guess I have, Mr. Frost. You see, I don't know how else to get up to the thirty-first floor.

Mr. Frost: Allen, you should use the executive elevator. That's what it's there for.

Allen: I didn't know there was an executive elevator!

Mr. Frost: Of course. When you came in here, you were given a set of keys. One of them is for the executive elevator. It really is beneath your position to be riding the elevator with the employees. I'll have my secretary instruct you about this.

Allen: OK, Mr. Frost. I'll be glad to have her show me where the gilded cage is. But, I've got to level with you. I doubt that I'll use it all the time. I feel I can get to know the people I'm working with when I'm squeezed into that little box with them, just eleven of them and me. So, if you don't mind, I'll probably be there with the other sardines.

Mr. Frost: Allen, I'm surprised at this reaction of yours. I'll have to consider it. Don't you realize that's one of the privileges that goes with your title here?

Allen: I'm afraid I look upon *that* as a responsibility. I feel it's a *privilege* to look at those cute secretaries in the morning. Sorta starts my day right.

Mr. Frost: I appreciate your candor on this, Allen. I just don't know.

Allen: Thanks for telling me about the key. I really didn't know anything about it.

EVALUATION

It's unfair to be upset with the performance of someone, or the lack thereof, when they aren't aware of what they should or shouldn't be doing. That's trap setting, an unfair form of game hunting. Bait for the trap?—Not leveling!

Know thyself

Good management begins with Socrates' admonition, "Know thyself." Unless we gain insight into ourselves to learn what motivates *us*, what *our* needs are, *our* prejudices, experiences, and so forth, is it possible for us to understand others? We must level with ourselves first.

In *Behind the Executive Mask*,[10] Dr. Alfred J. Morrow states it this way:

> Self-knowledge is a business necessity if the manager is to develop the cooperative relationships which will turn his subordinates into a working team with good morale and high motivation.
>
> A first step, therefore, is for the man who manages others to take a good close look at himself; to follow the ancient precept to "know thyself." He must examine his attitudes, recognize his inadequacies and failings, and then reshape them into new insights and skills. This discovery and reshaping of the self is at the heart of that re-education which management needs today.

Once we possess some insight into our *self*, it's important to face the facts squarely, even the unpleasant ones, in an endeavor to capitalize on our strengths and minimize our weaknesses. We must believe in our own capabilities. If we don't like ourselves, it's difficult to be truly creative, it's difficult to succeed. If we like ourselves, then others are more apt to like us, others are more apt to respect us.

Why pretend to be what we aren't? Due to our backgrounds we are all conditioned to attempt to *please* people. It may be much more important to just "do your own thing." Others will like us more without our masks. *Be yourself!* Remember, the only things a mature manager is responsible for are the choices he makes and their consequences. Leveling with yourself, your consequences will be easier to live with, and so will your future.

Start by leveling with yourself. We can't completely level with someone else until we've leveled with ourselves. Ask yourself:

"Is this really an issue I should get involved in? Or should it be my boss' concern, and should I tell him?"

"Do I really have a legitimate bone to pick, or do I just want to put him down?"

"Am I really convinced that his attitude is bad for the team?"

"What's the payoff? What's at stake?"

"How will he react? What will it take to get my point across?"

Before encountering someone, question your motives and what's at stake by being honest with yourself. You'll be better able to direct the dialogue the way it should go. Sometimes, when we're honest with ourselves we find the price is too high to engage in a discussion, or we're doing it just to please our own ego. When we know our motives, we know where *we* are headed. Then we'll be better equipped to manage and direct others.

First, though, you must be comfortable with yourself. You must know what *you* want for *you*, then proceed. Pick out the people you like and who like you *as you are*. You're not going to like everyone and everyone isn't going to like you. Don't try to please everyone; just be yourself and they'll like you for what you are, not for what you're trying to make yourself for them.

Level. It's more comfortable. Deceive and it's rough to live with. James Whitcomb Riley wrote, "Oh, what a tangled web we weave when first we practice to deceive." Being devious for ulterior motives doesn't pay off in the short or long run, especially if you're discovered. You stand to lose *all!* With yourself, with others, honesty is the best policy.

Accomplishing change through leveling

Since a major problem of management is a breakdown in communications between the manager and his employees, management has taken a look at a new technique in dialogue called the rap sessions. The object of such a session is to locate pertinent problems and effect necessary changes. Germane to each session is the basic premise that there must be total leveling and honesty between the participants. Management and employees meet to *level* with each other. Candor is the keynote of a rap session. Social and business amenities are scrapped. Openness and informality are the order—it's a family affair to hash over problem areas and obtain suggestions for change and growth.

The results of these sessions are almost always a revelation. Employees get the feeling that *management cares* about them. The leveling serves to defuse tensions that could be potential bombs. Creative ideas for change flow freely in the atmosphere of group sharing.

These ideas can improve products, increase production, and raise profits. The honesty factor enriches the understanding and satisfaction of everyone involved.

When we're leveling we can't hide behind establishment apron strings. The classic is the fellow who doesn't want to face facts. He can always put into the fire that old chestnut, "But it's against company policy." This is the oldest copout in the managerial handbook. It stops dialogue, or at best, jams the smooth flow toward seeking solutions to problems, toward effecting change. *Rare* are the times when a manager should hide behind this shield. Better he faces the facts and allows action to begin. The greatest risk he runs in using this phrase is that he invariably sets a trap for himself. He now is a huge nonmoving target for passive resistance on the part of the group. They will probably set out to prove to him that the company policy is absolute, and it's the policy that needs changing.

Then there are the hinge-heads. A hinge-head has his head on a hinge; it has only one way to go, up and down. Sometimes he's referred to as a "yes man." He's the person to whom it seems most important to be liked or to get along. Others may like him, but when the truth is known, he isn't respected since he never takes a stand on anything. To gain respect it's necessary to level, to be honest, to display candor. Leveling doesn't obliterate the possibility of respect, it nurtures it. A subordinate should feel free to disagree with his manager, to come to him with problems, to level with him on a healthy one-to-one basis. Hinge-heading is a sure sign of a person whose primary interest is *self, not company!* He contributes little if anything to creativity and change.

Employees complain, "My boss will never level with me. How do I find out how I'm doing, how they see me, and what I can do to change and improve?" If a manager doesn't level with his subordinates, peers, and upper management, it's difficult for change to be effected. *"How can I change if I don't know what needs changing?"* Len experiences this in the following case:

Case Study No. 10 / I'm the BOSS!

Len is a young man, vibrant, full of new ideas. He has just completed his first six months as a supervisor in a large production plant. He's attending his regular Monday morning meeting with his boss, Norman. The meeting is under way.

Norman: Well, Len, things look bad! I've been trying to keep this from you, but things look bad.

Len: Whadda-ya-mean, bad?

Norman: Well, I've been trying to spare you this, but since you've been here, production in your area has decreased steadily. We can't let this go on. Since your seniority is lowest, I'm going to have to let you go.

Len: You've gotta be kidding. Why didn't you tell me before? I didn't know this. I knew it wasn't too good, but——FIRED!

PROBLEM

Although it's good to get to the act of execution swiftly, Norman was really Charles Addams about it. Obviously, this was the first Norman had mentioned to Len about production. Norman had not leveled with him. Len was unaware of his impending doom, yet Norman gave him no time for self-defense.

POSSIBLE SOLUTION

Norman: Well, Len, I've got some fact sheets that should be meaningful to you. They're for your first six months here.

Len: OK, let's have it. I have an idea that they don't read as good as I'd like.

Norman: Then you've sensed it too?

Len: I know production isn't where it should be, and I know I don't feel comfortable among the men any more. Can you level with me? What's happening here?

Norman: Well, let's take things as they've happened. When you first came on the job, what was your attitude toward the men when you'd come into the plant in the morning?

Len: Well, I spoke to them.

Norman: Let me level with you, Len. When I hired you you were alive with enthusiasm. At that point, I figured nothing could stop you. Then I saw a change in you the first day you walked on the job. Do you know what I mean?

Len: I think I do, Norman. I felt like I was the supervisor, that I shouldn't be too friendly with the men. I guess I didn't think it fit the title. I felt like they were established here, that we were sorta in competition. Now that you've mentioned this, I realize I've been damned unfriendly.

Norman: You're getting the message. What rules did you change when you started? Rules that dealt with the daily activities of the men?

Len: Well, I figured to get them to respect me I'd have to crack down on some of their laxity. We enforced the time limit for coffee breaks, and we cut out personal phone calls. And we enforced no smoking while working.

Norman: We? You mean, I.

Len: Yeah, I didn't ask them, I *told* them!

Norman: Did these things make the people respond for you, Len?

Len: At first I thought they were working. I thought I had things under control. Lately, I have my doubts.

Norman: How many friends do you have among your immediate subordinates?

Len: None! I really didn't think I was out to win any sort of friendship contest. I don't talk with the men except when the job demands it.

Norman: Is that a comfortable feeling for you?

Len: Not really, not at all. I think I've goofed! I came here with lots of preconceived notions about what a manager's role should be. Now, you're telling me production is down and I'm beginning to see why.

Norman: I like the Len I see in front of me now, and the guy I hear talking to me now. He sounds like the man I hired six months ago. How can you transfer this to your men?

Len: I'd like to wipe out the last six months. I'd like to go down there right now and tell them what an ass I've been and bend over and let them kick me. I don't think that'd get the job done either.

Norman: What do you think *would* get the job done?

Len: It has to be gradual. I'll start with saying hello in the morning. And I'm going to return those personal privileges I took away from them. How stupid can I be, trying to dictate whether or not they'll have that extra cigarette? If they're going to smoke they'll smoke, anyway. I was just using that as an excuse to show my weight.

Norman: Do you think this'll help production?

Len: I'm gonna give it a helluva try and see! I want to know more about these guys. I want to get their thinking on lots of ideas.

Norman: What you're telling me is, you want to go back to your section and relate to the men on more friendly terms, forgetting about the image of what management should be like. Right?

Len: Right! I'd like to come back here next Monday with new facts and figures about an increase in production, and a better relationship with those men. If you'll give me another six months, I'll prove myself. With the help of those guys, I—WE—can top the production figures of the day I walked in here!

Norman: That's the spirit. I like your enthusiasm! Now, let's see you prove it—turn it into production!

EVALUATION

With Norman's guidance, it appears that Len's on the right track. As a result, this episode has decreased turnover by one. It saved training a replacement, and chances are that after this discussion Len will be a valuable employee.

When you don't know what's objectionable about your performance or behavior, it really is difficult to change. Unless someone levels with you, the only way to recognize your inadequacies is as people begin to reject your company. You'll be the forced loner in every group.

What was once decided can be undecided. Things can be changed! We have the freedom to change, yet this freedom exists only through knowing the truth about ourselves and about others. Then we can exercise the blessed gift of our freedom to change. When we possess the facts, then we can make decisions. But when we have to make decisions on partial facts, the decisions are more difficult and may be incorrect.

The choice is ours as to whether or not we change, but at least when we know our faults and we choose to do something about them—to change—we'll know what needs changing.

The emotional side of leveling

1. *Warehousing:* What happens to the emotions when we don't level, when we choose to keep things pent-up inside? People who don't level have to pay the penalty of emotional divorce. Failure to level with each other can lead to totally unexpected dramatic crisis.

Numerous studies point up that over a long period of time it can cause traumatic psychogenic ailments such as ulcers, migraine headaches, backaches, shingles, and other disorders. To prevent paying such high prices for containing our emotions, it's better to "let it hit the fan!" There can be no mature meaningful relationship without leveling. This may or may not take the form of loud voices. It's less apt to be demonstrated this way if it's vented as it happens or shortly thereafter, rather than accumulating it in a worry-warehouse, then shipping it all out at once. *Have it out as it happens. Speak up! Say what's eating you.* Negotiate for realistic settlements of differences. It may be briefly painful but it's easier once the problem is verbalized. We have to learn to level, so when something gets to you, verbalize it! It won't just go away! Your subconscious remembers it even if your conscious doesn't. Then, when your emotional warehouse fills, it's dangerous—it has to overflow sooner or later. What's the payoff for all of this? In *Behind the Executive Mask*,[11] Dr. Morrow answers this question in the form of some feedback from a member of a T-group:

> It's amazing how many things I had been building up inside me that I wanted to say and yet never opened up about. . . . At home and on the job I wouldn't think of admitting any weaknesses. Yet it is these very secret weaknesses that cause us to worry about losing our jobs or our promotions. If we could only talk these things out instead of keeping our fears to ourselves—if the people we work with could only develop enough confidence to "let go," we'd straighten out a lot of problems we never even dared to admit existed.
>   . . . I learned that unless I was willing to stick my neck out, I was going to have to give up any hopes of a leadership position in the T-group because I had nothing to offer.

2. *Can I trust you?:* "Can I trust you?" That's a question we should ask when we know someone who's always in control of his emotions, who constantly wears a smile on his face, and is always in agreement. He's the same as sun and water. Like sun he's welcome and enjoyed, but an overdose causes drought; things burn and become arid. Like water it's pleasurable, cleansing, and purifying, but left without change, it becomes stagnant and polluted. It takes a balance of smiles and a few frowns to display a healthy emotional outlook, to be believable, to establish trust.

The best results in behavior development come when an employer and employee get together and argue. That's right, *argue!* (Politely, this is termed "heated negotiations.") If there isn't argument, there isn't growth. Each must know what the subject area is about; each takes his position and the dialogue is on. They air their views, summarize the points made, then proceed toward reconciliation. It's better to have some hurt feelings briefly than to have a malignant relationship. It's a fallacy that peace and harmony in an organization are signs of a healthy group. To the contrary, they're red-flag warnings of a crisis that may be about to explode.

Let's see what Walter did, in his fantasy, as a result of being "peaceful":

Walter is the quiet, soft-spoken vice president of a small successful plastics company. He's a pillar of the community and helper in many charitable causes. He has a reputation of having never been heard to say a cross word, ever, to anyone. His philosophy revolves around the bromide, "If you can't say something good about someone, don't say anything at all."

Walter's president is a dynamic leader. He's strong physically, and mentally, he's a genius. He leads with deftness and finality. He's never in doubt about anything and speaks with authority and intellect. Walter has been his second in command for many years. People have often commented how well they complement each other. They're a balance in their strengths and weaknesses. Walter has great respect for his president and treats him with like accord.

One day, the sun is shining into Walter's office. It hits across his desk and reflects up into his glasses. Momentarily, he's mesmerized. He muses to himself what's in his subconscious mind:

"I've held it all inside myself for all of the fourteen years and twenty-six days that I've worked with this domineering tyrant. I've been his faithful dog, at his beck and call. I've jumped to his slightest command. I've cleaned up after him when he'd get in too deep. I've alibied for him—yes, even lied for him. I've hated every minute of these fourteen years and twenty-six days with him. Now, it's MY turn!

"I'm going to show him. I'm going to sandbag that bastard, then it's my turn.

"Let's see now, I'll ask him to go fishing with me for the weekend. I know he can't swim. When we're out in the middle of the deep quiet lake—*ZAP!* I'll pull the plug out of the bottom of the boat; then I'll leap out and swim out of his reach. As the boat slowly sinks, treading water I'll look back. I'll yell all the dastardly things this ape has done to me. I'll invoke the curses of the gods on him.

"And as the boat and its passenger slowly sink beneath the surface, I'll wave good-by to the sonofabitch whose seat I'll then occupy as president of the company!"

What was Walter's problem? Failure to level. Daydreaming is a safety valve for tension and anxiety, but it's a temporary substitute for leveling. The emotions are still there and must be dealt with eventually.

It's dangerous to keep everything inside oneself. Just as it was Walter's way to sandbag his boss, so there's a boiling point for everyone where we must express our intense feelings. Better to say them openly as they're being felt. If we warehouse them, eventually they'll explode, perhaps in a sandbagging episode such as Walter's.

3. *Acknowledge Anger:* The New Testament states, "Let not the sun go down upon thy wrath."

Be willing to express anger. It's helpful to do this, but you must be willing to stand still for someone to unload their anger back at you. It may take the form of shouting or quiet anger, but whichever, *let it out, clear the air! Anger blocks both reason and logic!*

Subtle sabotage can take place if the anger isn't expressed. Consciously or subconsciously, people make the mistake of repressing anger. If anger is expressed right along, it won't be warehoused to cause hurt pride. Hurt pride often evidences itself as rage; it's better to dissipate anger early.

As children our parents trained us to repress feelings of anger. You remember when they said, "Now don't you get mad!" That was the beginning. It's become a conditioned response for us over many years to suppress strong emotions. Now, we must learn to reverse the process, to level!

When we demand of ourselves that we remain in total control we may be asking too much of ourselves. Anger is normal and healthy. Anger is a good emotion and should *not* be distorted. The violent man is really the man who's too much in control too often. When he's warehoused his anger for many years, it's apt to be violent when it finally explodes. Anger expressed as it's experienced is replaced by a warm, healthy feeling. Then a relationship can continue, can grow.

The sooner anger is recognized, the better. We may repress anger subconsciously, not even knowing it's there. Subsequently, it's necessary for us to learn to recognize it, to let it out. If we collect anger over a long period of time until it builds rage, this can terminate a job for us very abruptly, or subtle sabotage may ensue. Unfortunately, managers feel that by repressing anger they can effect good communications, but it doesn't work that way. Say it! Clear the air! When we're actively angry and fail to vent our anger, we reach the point where we hear virtually not a word being said to us. It's better to siphon anger through dialogue; then we'll be able to hear. Lower the temperature of emotions through dialogue, so you'll be able to function properly.

Getting angry tells the other person, "I care about you or I wouldn't get angry. I respect you enough to be honest with you and for you to be honest with me. I have confidence in you and our relationship. I'll take what you have to say and you take what I have to say so we can clear the air."

> I was angry with my friend:
> I told my wrath, my wrath did end.
> I was angry with my foe:
> I told it not, my wrath did grow.

The leveling game

Most people are game players. Many of the games we play are uncomfortable people-games we'd love to stop playing. We lead a camouflaged life when we indulge in daily people-games. It's tiring and anxiety arousing. People engaging in these games never really know where they're at. The more skillful they are, the less they know, since their objective is to not be known and not to have their motives discovered. Result: They don't know who they are themselves. The goal of such people-games is to trick the opponent into doing what you want them to do. Players of people-games live lives shrouded with doubt, suspicion, anxiety, uncertainty, and fear. Human beings aren't equipped to withstand these pressures for

extended periods of time without suffering emotionally and physically. We can stop playing anxiety games by using candor, through
leveling. Let's replace the anxiety game with a new one, the leveling
game. These are the ground rules:

1. When leveling, you must level about ideas, not about people; at
behavior, not at the person.

2. Direct your remarks to the person who is at fault, not to just
anyone. If your gripe is with your boss, level with him, not your
partner.

3. Avoid holding someone else up as the shining example. Com-
parisons with others who are "better" will disintegrate self-esteem.
The listener will probably tune out when this happens.

4. Seek privacy for your encounter. It's demeaning to have peers
tuned in on your leveling session.

5. Put the harp away. Once you've made your point, don't keep
bringing it up repetitiously and harping on it.

6. Don't let the fire smolder. If you're irritated about something,
say so as quickly as possible. The longer you postpone this "un-
savory task," the more you tend to distort the facts and make assumptions for the other person.

7. Forgive and forget! Once you've leveled about a particular
point and it's understood, go onward! Otherwise, it's like a parent
shaming the child by admonishing him repetitiously. Say it—drop it
—forget it!

8. Level about only one major issue at a time. Air gripes as they
occur; then there'll usually be only one major topic to discuss at any
one time.

9. Level about things that can be changed. It's possible to change
a habit—the length of time taken for coffee breaks, for example—
but it's difficult to change a habit of worrying.

10. Avoid hedging around about what's to be said. Get to the point
quickly; it's less painful that way. *Say it!* Feel the relief? It's almost
instant!

11. Forget apologies when leveling. Once you've made your point,
don't apologize for it. Apology has its place only when you're really
wrong about something. Then be an adult and admit it!

12. Scuttle sarcasm. It doesn't belong in leveling or anyplace else
in dialogue. It's childish and creates a bitter reaction.

13. Look 'em in the eye! When you level, look at the person; it's

an indication of integrity. If you're right in what you're saying, you *can* look 'em in the eye!

14. Are your nerves showing? Do you have the fidgets? Stop. These habits weaken your point and your position. They can lose stature and credibility for you.

15. Offer an alternate recommendation when you level with someone. Better still, ask them to offer what they feel would be a better way.

16. Leave with an encouraging conclusion—"I know you can do it," for example. This is more desirable than the parental admonition, "If you don't shape up, you'll have to ship out!"

The leveling game isn't concluded until its participants feed back objections to insure that both players are talking about the same things. Semantics can destroy true meaning, so feed back by paraphrasing. Once understanding is established, an attempt to evolve a course of action can be undertaken. It's a serious and delicate thing to be leveled at.

Leveling has these synonyms: sincerity, frankness, openness, honesty, truthfulness. If you can be these things, first with yourself and then with others, you'll be able to enjoy better interpersonal communications and avoid the ulcer clan.

Carlyle sums it up: "Can there be a more horrible object in existence than an eloquent man not speaking the truth?"

Leveling is an art—it must be learned. It's one of the manager's greatest arbitrators, well worth learning. It stands to gain him respect, trust, and confidence—without which he cannot be an effective leader or manager.

AVOID PASSIVITY

All of us become passive in our dialogue at some time, to a greater or lesser degree. This is normal. When we become passive we refuse involvement in conversation or we engage in it on a cursory level. When this happens, it's impossible to resolve matters of depth or importance. For conversation to be virile and zestful, passivity must be avoided by all concerned.

What is passivity? *It's failure to become involved. It's fear of becoming involved, of letting others know us, of knowing others. It's apathy, lethargy, sullenness. It's death to dialogue. The opposite of love isn't hate, it's passivity.* If we love, we want others to know us and we want to know others, to become involved, to understand each other. The opposite of this is passivity, where we decline serious verbal intercourse with others.

A man once bragged that he'd figured out how to handle his bosses. This was a "giant" statement—Eureka, the magic formula! What was his secret? He put it this way: "Well, I just agree with them about whatever they say, then I do as I please, do what *I* want to." This is a classic attitude of a passive person. The man wouldn't express himself to his bosses, he would just "hinge-head" with them, then do what he wanted. He wouldn't become involved!

What's caused passivity to be so much a part of our society— Society itself! As in leveling, we were trained to be passive both as children and adolescents. Society nurtured our early conditioning of apathy. Remember those good old cliches: "Children should be seen and not heard" . . . "Hear no evil, see no evil, speak no evil" . . . "If you can't say something good about someone, don't say anything at all" . . . "Why stick your neck out?" . . . "Don't ask questions!" The number of cliches is irrelevant. They all instilled the same attitudes: "Peace at any price," and "Don't stir the water; maybe it'll all go away!" Sociologically we were conditioned to be passive. We've been brought up on "Let George do it!" and "Silence is golden!"

Recently a manager read this quotation: "The dogmas of the quiet past are insufficient to the present struggle." His reaction was "How true, our apathy won't take care of our problems today." He read on to learn that the author of the quotation was Abraham Lincoln. Ours isn't the only generation plagued by this syndrome. It's an age-old problem.

Why are people passive? Fear is the great breeder of passivity. We fear rejection. We want people to like us. We're afraid to speak up for fear of being rejected. We fear being misunderstood. We fear appearing to be troublemakers. Certainly we don't want people to think we're weak and complaining, so we'll suffer in passive silence rather than speak out to be heard.

The strongest, most aggressive person becomes passive under certain stimuli. If the payoff isn't there, we're apt to become apathetic. When trivia is the topic, we may see no payoff in involvement, so we'll resort to being nonparticipative. There are times when we "just can't stand that bastard." As a result, when we have to be in his company, we'll become passive. A person who just doesn't "dig" dirty stories becomes apathetic when in the company of prolific dirty-joke tellers. All of us have our times for withdrawing from participation in dialogue, when we're passive.

What happens to dialogue when it involves a passive person? The incident of *Presto! Three Hundred Bodies*, indicates how relations can disintegrate when passivity is involved.

Case Study No. 11 / Presto! Three Hundred Bodies

Bill Hill is personnel manager of a large mill. One day he walks into the office of his supervisor, Ted Page. Bill puts his resignation on Ted's desk. Ted reads: "Effective two weeks from today, please accept my resignation due to situations with which I am unable to cope. Thank you. William Hill."

Ted: What's this, Bill, your resignation from the company?

Bill: That's right. I'm quitting.

Ted: But your resignation simply says "due to situations with which I am unable to cope." What the heck do you mean by that?

Bill: Let's forget it. I'm quitting, that's that!

Ted: Well, if you feel that way about your job and the company, it sure wouldn't be to our advantage to have you around. You said two weeks' notice? Why don't you go by the paymaster right now? I'll call and tell them to make out a two-week advance severance check for you. No point you sticking around if that's your attitude.

Bill: You're right, Ted. No point my sticking around. I'm so fed up now, I don't think I could take it here another two weeks, anyhow!

PROBLEM

The company has lost a four-year employee. They'll have to seek and train a new personnel manager.

Bill is full of resentment. It hasn't been drained off. It's a safe bet he won't have anything complimentary to say about either Ted or the company.

Ted still doesn't know what caused Bill to quit. Will he be able to control a similar situation in the future? Not until it evidences itself again through a new personnel manager.

The situation has deteriorated to the point that it probably *is*

better for Bill to leave. Why? Because he still has no lines of communication open to: a) solve his problem, b) have healthy dialogue
with Ted.

ALTERNATE APPROACH

Ted: What's this, Bill, your resignation from the company?

Bill: That's right, I'm quitting.

Ted: But your resignation simply says "due to situations with
which I'm unable to cope." I didn't know anything was wrong. Can
you tell me what these "situations" are?

Bill: It won't do any good to talk about it. I've made up my mind.

Ted: I respect your right to resign, Bill. If that's your final decision, I'll abide by it. I regret losing you. You've done a great job
here. It'll be tough to replace you. But even if you decide to go
through with this, it would help me to know why you feel the need
to resign.

Bill: We've been good friends. It isn't anything personal.

Ted: Then, can you tell me what these situations are? They must
have something to do with the company and its policies or working
conditions.

Bill: OK. You're asking for it. I'm fed up with this lack of communication between production and personnel. Someone "up there"
decides to increase production. They order materials to do this and
the next thing I know I'm supposed to have three hundred more
employees to work the machines to meet their production forecast!
They never ask me if it's *possible to get* three hundred more employees to run those machines! They never ask me if I have it in
my budget to salary that many more people! They never consider
how long it'll take to train that many new people! It seems to me
they just expect me to push some magic button and *PRESTO!* Three
hundred bodies! The people will be there turning out the product.
It doesn't work that way, Ted!

Ted: OK. OK, Bill! I hear you! I hear your frustrations, too! I
didn't realize forecast ideas weren't being exchanged between your
department and production. You've always come up with the personnel in the past. I suppose I just sat here with my eyes closed to
anything beneath this fact. How long has this been going on?

Bill: It was going on when I came here four years ago. I thought
it would work itself out. But it hasn't and I'm fed up!

Ted: Wait a minute, Bill. I recognize your frustration. I hear lots of confusion and resentment, too, at not being considered in the overall production planning. Of course, *your* department is *vital* to meeting any forecast. What do you think we can do to correct this situation?

Bill: Let me in on what's going on! When the big wheels sit down to project next year's production needs, let me have my say about whether or not I'll be able to get the people to produce for them.

Ted: That sounds simple, Bill. Sure isn't an unreasonable thing to accomplish. Do you think it'd make life easier for you if we'd have a meeting of production and personnel? We can open this up for discussion. We'll include you *and your thinking* in future meetings!

Bill: That'd be great! But I've already told you, I'm quitting.

Ted: Yes, you've told *me.* But I haven't told anyone else. If you'd be willing to give it another try, I'd like to destroy this letter of resignation, with the understanding that in the future you'll be at all forecast meetings! And, with the understanding that when you're in a bind about things, you'll come in and talk them out before they get to this advanced state of crisis. Let's keep our lines of communication open.

Bill: Damn, why didn't I came in and talk this over with you before? It all sounds so simple, Ted, to just consider me and my department. Of course, that's the answer. I really don't want to quit here. I like this mill, and the people. What you said about keeping our lines of communication open—you may see me parked in your outer office more often. I always thought you were too busy to see me. I'll take my chances from now on. Thanks, Ted.

EVALUATION

Bill felt relieved at having vented his anger. His statement, "It all sounds so simple," sums it up. *To unload a complaint, to air it, is almost immediate relief from the tension and frustration. Then, and only then, can we think constructively.*

Characteristics of passivity

As a manager, it's important to be cognizant of some characteristics of passivity. These are the red flags of a passive person.

1. Really needs to be thought of as a "nice guy." *Fears rejection.*

2. Hypersensitive, he wears his feelings on his sleeve. He's housed in a very thin shell, easily penetrated by a cross word or a frown.

3. Needs acceptance, therefore wishes to please. Loves applause!

4. Looks for companions who are nonaggressive and talks in platitudes.

5. Others seldom know what he's really thinking. His fear is someone will reprimand him or disagree.

6. He's expert in ambiguities and irrelevancies. It's difficult to know where you stand with him.

7. Avoids arguments and walks away from differences of opinion.

8. Controversy upsets him. He'll take it as being directed at him. He wounds quickly and deeply.

9. Pride is fast hurt and slow healing. Bears a grudge ad infinitum.

10. Sees things as all black, all white. Deals in absolutes.

11. Since friction and hostility are his two greatest fears, he lives in a shell, away from serious dialogue and interaction with others and reality.

12. Slow to take action on decision.

There's an Arabian proverb, "All sunshine makes a desert." When in public the passive person disguises himself behind the mask of smiles. He hides his insecurity and feelings of inadequacy. He denies the reality of life, of pain and conflict, and as a result, he tunes out matters of depth and importance. Usually this person is thought of as being extremely polite, and he is. However, this is a facade to camouflage his personal insecurities and his more intense emotions.

Why should a manager be concerned with this person in his midst? He can be trouble in many ways. Not only does he refrain from contributing to creativity and understanding, but he can be a sandbagger, too, as we'll see in the following instance.

A group of production workers were uptight about their foreman because he was showing favoritism to one of the employees. In numerous ways, it was obvious their relationship was more than just casual.

The workers decided to unite and reduce their production to the point where the foreman's record would be questioned. As a result, he would either be transferred from the department, or someone would investigate the decrease in production. He might even be fired! The workers figured, at least they'd have the opportunity to air their grievances.

The problem here was passivity on the part of the workers; to not openly discuss their grievance. Instead of talking it out, they kept it passively within their group and decided to sandbag the foreman. With their silence, and by reducing their production, they would accomplish their goal!

A gripe that isn't aired can become a grievance, can become a disaster! The time for the group to express their feelings was when they openly recognized agreement about the foreman's favoritism. In this instance, passivity precipitated poor production.

What stirs the wrath of the passive person? Usually it has to do with his feeling exploited, dominated, or being treated in an undignified way.

Negative manifestations

The negative side of passivity displays itself in many forms. Seldom would we consider them open or noticeable. To the contrary, they take the form of subtle subterfuge, sulking, and silence.

1. *Silent Treatment:* The manager may misinterpret these signs at first. The silent treatment isn't cooperation or strength, it's hostility camouflaged by phony and misleading compliance. "Golden silence" only leads to a hopelessness of any personal relationship other than platitudes. When complaints aren't aired, they can erupt in a total fiasco where the person just "packs up and walks away," as did Bill in *Presto, Three Hundred Bodies.* Rather than cause controversy about an issue, it's easier for the passive person to just pack up and leave.

2. *Double-talk:* Another manifestation of passivity is withholding information. This person doesn't directly refuse to answer a manager's questions; he merely answers in a roundabout manner, or he avoids the mention of issues that would be illuminating to the subject under discussion. He may not do this maliciously, but he just forgets to include the matter in conversation. He'll double-talk about many irrelevancies and he's adept at sidetracking your thinking to another issue.

Nearly all those who indulge in double-talking will think they have tried to voice their real thinking, their objections or contributions, and weren't listened to. They've done such a good job at camouflage, they've confused their listeners *and* themselves. Any complaining they'd do would be encased in so much double-talk and vagueness that the point becomes obscure.

3. *Passive Resistance:* When encountering someone who is aggressive and decisive, the passive person best shows *his* strength through *passive resistance. The more delaying he does, the more dominant he becomes.* If a manager suggests repeatedly that some action be taken, the longer the passive person resists taking action, the stronger he becomes. He's telling the manager, "See who's more important. I am! I won't do what you're telling me to do until *I get ready to.* That'll show you who's more important! *I am!"*

Passive resistance is a manifestation of anger. When this is displayed, a manager probably doesn't know it until it's too late. It takes the form of apathy, refusal to contribute thinking or ideas to the group activities, resistance to change, failure to comply with suggestions, etc.

Passivity begets passivity

When a person is passive, he puts others in a position where they have to make decisions for him. He just doesn't act! By his inaction, when things have to be done, his associates are forced to make decisions for him and to take action without him. As a result he develops a feeling of being domineered or left out. He resents this. So, he decides to go into silence. In turn his associates conclude that if he doesn't want to get involved they'll leave him alone. So, they decide to go into silence. His passivity begets passivity. It's like children saying, "If you don't want to play ball with me, then I won't play ball with you!"

In business, we sometimes have to pay a price for our passivity since, indeed, it does beget passivity. *What Happened Here While I Was Gone* suggests the meaning to this statement.

Case Study No. 12 / What Happened Here While I Was Gone!

Brad Taylor is assistant purchasing agent for a hardwood manufacturing company. He's just returned from a convention and has asked to see Alan Wellington, company vice president, and his friend.

Alan: Well, Brad, how was the convention?

Brad: The usual.

Alan: Do you have the reports from the meetings?

Brad: Yes, they're right here.

Alan: Everything going OK?

Brad: Yes. I'll leave the reports with your Secretary. Unless you want to talk them now.

Alan: No, that'll be fine. We'll lunch one of these days?

Brad: Sure.

PROBLEM

Did Brad have a problem? If so, he passively avoided mentioning it to Alan. The talk was light, but tense.

ALTERNATE APPROACH

Alan: Well, Brad, how was the convention?

Brad: The usual. But it's what happened here while I way away! Hell! I'm really burned-up!

Alan: Can you be more specific, Brad?

Brad: You know damned good and well what I mean, Alan. Who's the outsider you brought in as my boss? I was in line for that promotion. Then, while I'm gone you bring someone in without even talking it with me. I'm pretty bitter right now.

Alan: I understand your feelings, Brad. Let's see if I can explain. We felt someone from the outside could bring fresh ideas with him.

Brad: (Interrupting) What you're saying is, my ideas aren't any good anymore.

Alan: Recently, Brad, you haven't contributed. You've been at several meetings where you were noncommittal and uninvolved.

Brad: One reason I haven't contributed, I didn't think anyone was listening to what I was saying.

Alan: We listened, but didn't always implement your suggestions.

Brad: I felt I was being "frozen-out"—not wanted on the team anymore. So, I quit sharing my ideas.

Alan: And when you did that, we felt you weren't "with us." We assumed you were either worn-out or didn't care. You know we base promotions on performance. So we brought in an outsider for the job.

Brad: Right now, all I'm hearing is we were doing each other's thinking. We weren't verbalizing our feelings, any of us. And this mess is the result.

Alan: I go along with that. We thought for you—you thought for us.

Brad: What bugs me too, you brought this man in while I was gone—behind my back.

Alan: That was a matter of coincidence, Brad. Very unintentional. How do you feel about working with him?

Brad: I'll work with him, Alan, of course. I like the company. I don't want to leave. But I *am* interested in advancing. I *do* want to take an active part in the "team."

All I can say is, I helped create this situation. Damn it, why didn't I tell you what I was feeling?

Alan: Let's try to have better communication in the future. Thanks for leveling, Brad.

Brad: It's easier that way.

EVALUATION

Both Alan and Brad have been passive in their attitudes. Passivity begets passivity. One being noncommittal produced like response on the part of the other. It's better to make known ones feelings as they're happening. As Brad said, "It's easier that way."

The bitching boss

Why are some bosses given this label? Why do some individuals say, "Nag, nag, nag—that's all my wife and my boss ever do! Every place I go, I meet a nagger! I'm so tired of being bitched at!" What causes nagging? Why do people nag? When you meet a person who is a nagger, you can bet that they're associated with a passive person. If a boss is labeled a griping, nagging so-and-so, it's usually because the employee who says this about him is passive. An employer has to mention ten times to an employee that he should do a specified task, then after the eleventh time, in despair, the employer does it himself. This is a form of passive resistance on the part of the employee. He's really "showing his muscle" when he doesn't comply with the employer's request within a reasonable length of time.

Acceptable rule: When a specific reasonable act is asked of you and you're capable of performing it, it's unfair not to do so within a reasonable or specified time. When you don't, you're exercising passive resistance and you can expect to be bitched at. No one is born a nagger; they're made that way by association with a passive person. When communications break down and passive resistance takes over, nagging begins.

The more you force communication with the passively resistant person, the harder you push to dialogue, the more he pulls away from you and tunes you out. In essence he stands there saying to himself, "Rave on, I'm not going to listen to you and I'm not going to answer you either, so just go on talking to yourself!" His indifference ignites frustration and anger. Eventually the relationship deteriorates and finally dies.

How to deal with passivity

Recognizing passivity, whether in ourselves or in others, is the first step to take in dealing with the problem. It's such a concealed thing, it hides skillfully. Therefore, it must first be recognized, then it can be dealt with.

If passivity is a major part of your way of life, once you've recognized it take action to correct it. Get involved! If you have an eye on a possible job opening, say so! It might never occur to your employer that you'd be interested in enrolling in advanced-training courses, or shifting from one capacity to another. Make your wishes known—"Knock and the door will open!"

Let's take the following passive attitudes and reverse them to active attitudes.

Passive	Active
Lack of thinking	To think
Lack of interest	To become interested
Lack of concern	To show concern
Lack of intellect	To demonstrate intelligence
Lack of respect	To verbalize respect
Lack of concentration	To concentrate
Lack of team spirit	To activate team spirit
Lack of cooperation	To cooperate

Let's see how many of these qualities evidence themselves in the following case:

Case Study No. 13 / Let's Not

At lunch three managers are talking about a forthcoming meeting. The purpose of this meeting is to evaluate training procedures. Discussion at this point is directed toward Jack, a fourth manager who would probably be at the meeting.

Larry: I don't think we should include Jack. He never has much to say.

Pat: I never know what he's thinking. I'm suspicious of someone who doesn't tell me where he stands.

Les: This guy? He joined the company sixteen months ago and I still can't figure out where he stands.

Pat: Let's not ask him to the meeting. We can get along without his thinking.

Les: He never expresses it, anyway. Why have him there?

Larry: We can tell him what's happened. That's good enough.

PROBLEM

Passivity. These three managers are refusing to include Jack because of his lack of involvement with them. For some reason, Jack is passive and doesn't express his feelings. We have to look at these three managers, too, as being passive. Are they attempting to understand Jack? How could the situation accomplish better understanding among the four men?

ALTERNATE APPROACH

Larry: I don't think we should include Jack. He never has much to say.

Pat: I never know what he's thinking. I'm suspicious of someone who doesn't tell me where he stands.

Les: Wait a minute, fellows. I agree with you about Jack's silence, but I'm not sure we have the right to exclude him from our meeting. He's on equal rank with us. It doesn't seem good business to leave him out of our training discussion.

Pat: That's true, Les, but it's an uncomfortable feeling, having someone just sitting there, not contributing any ideas, just sitting!

Larry: I wonder what's inside that guy's head? He seems to do a good job. People like him, but I can't share that feeling.

Les: I'm uncomfortable, too, when I'm around Jack. I wonder why he doesn't open up with us?

Lerry: Maybe we should confront him about this. I'd like to have better rapport with him. After all, he should be a member of our team. If we really open up to him about the way we feel, he might come around to join us.

Les: Wait a minute. I think you just hit it. Join *us!* We've worked together for almost ten years, the three of us. The three musketeers! Along comes Jack, the outsider. I have to admit, I haven't tried to make him a part of our group.

Pat: This hurts to admit, but I've made no effort other than casually asking him to be at our meetings.

Les: It could be our fault, Jack's not contributing to our conversation. We're a damned powerful group. All of us know how the others think, we can level with each other. I'd hate to have been in Jack's shoes these sixteen months, bucking US!

Pat: Let's ask him to lunch with us tomorrow. That's a beginning point.

Larry: Yeh! We've never even done that. We'll start there and tell him we've been talking today. Let's see if we can get him to level and develop some understanding.

Les: I'll call him when I get back to the office. We need Jack's ideas and his creativity. You know, he might say some damned smart things if we shut up long enough to give him the chance.

EVALUATION

Passivity is a defense. It's an attempt, in some way, to be as strong as others. Pat, Larry, and Les are a strong team. Jack joined the company long after they were well established. When they didn't include him in their group, he became silently passive. *His passivity has been his defense against their strength and against their rejection of him*—of their not allowing him to belong on their team. His need for belonging was thwarted and he resorted to passivity in self-defense.

It helps to attempt seeing and feeling as the other person might be seeing and feeling.

When we evaluate the alternate approach, we see that the men used all of the listed active attitudes previously mentioned. They began to *think*, they *became interested* in why Jack reacted as he did, and they *showed concern* for having isolated him. They *demonstrated intelligence* in attempting to realize how Jack has been feeling, and they *respected* his stance against the group's rejection. They *concentrated* on what would be a desirable path of action to *activate team spirit* to include Jack. They voted to *cooperate* to bring Jack into their circle.

It's a manager's responsibility to create an atmosphere in which others may be motivated to move from the passive to the active. Dialogue is your main avenue toward accomplishment of this responsibility. Your best approach is:

1. Avoid rationalizing and intellectualizing. This approach is of *no* value in exploding passivity.

2. Express understanding. For example, tell the person, "I feel you are frustrated by the events that have transpired. I understand your need for the new title," etc. Let him know that you understand what his problems are, what his needs age. Acknowledge these, but avoid being sympathetic and solicitous.

3. Make the person aware of his resistance. "You don't seem willing to accept my proposal. Is there something I've done, or that the company has done?"

4. Remain neutral. Don't take sides with him or with someone else. Remain in a mobile position. Be objective; keep personal opinions out of it.

5. Evaluate the other person's objections with him, his reservations. Draw him out. "You don't seem willing to discuss the matter further. Is there something I may have said to annoy you?"

"What are your reservations?" "What are your objections?" Any response to such questions in the form of an objection or explanation must be fully understood. Examine carefully, objectively.

6. If emotions get involved, be sure they belong to the other person, not to you. Keep your cool! Let *their* emotions flow; this is the best thing that can happen. Then, once emotions are detonated, you can proceed to a path of constructive thinking.

7. Attempt to resolve a mode of action that will develop and cultivate action on their part. Get them involved!

Now, Children demonstrates dealing with the passivity of Mr. Peterson who, in the first instance, is passive and, in the second instance, active.

Case Study No. 14 / Now, Children

Mr. Peterson is the manager of a metropolitan bank. He has observed one of his tellers arriving consistently late for the opening of business. He has called an early morning meeting of his thirty-eight employees. The meeting is just beginning:

Mr. Peterson: Good morning, ladies and gentlemen. I'm glad you are all in attendance this morning. Sometimes there are things that come to my attention that need to be discussed with the group. As you know, we have certain company policies that are strict and by which we must operate to stay in business. We have a fine group of people working here. You are very efficient, trustworthy, and pleasant employees. We look upon you as our family, with each dependent upon the other for survival. We want you to know how much your loyalty is appreciated and how important you are to the growth of our business. We have your cooperation on most every level and we are a number-one business because of this. We find, however, that there are times when there is tardiness on your time cards. We know this is occasionally unavoidable. We understand when there is some legitimate reason why you're late. We want to have the business open with full staff each morning promptly at 9:00 A.M. We look forward to all of you helping us to achieve this goal. And remember, we're like a strong chain, but we're only as strong as our weakest link. We know that YOU aren't going to be that one weak link. So, let's all pull together and return to your desks and windows now. We'll strive for EXCELLENCE! TEAM SPIRIT! You're dismissed.

PROBLEM

Mr. Peterson is passive in his approach to the problem of one employee's tardiness. Note—one, not all, of his employees. Yet, because of his passivity, he chooses not to face the one employee to discuss the problem with him. Instead, as in a parent-children relationship, he exposes the problem to the entire staff. His approach is the traditional "give praise before criticizing" technique.

ALTERNATE APPROACH

Let's put Mr. Peterson together with tardy Sam.

Mr. Peterson: Good morning, Sam.

Sam: Good morning, Mr. Peterson.

Mr. Peterson: I've pulled your file this morning, Sam, to discuss your standard-of-performance record.

Sam: It isn't time for that is it, Mr. Peterson?

Mr. Peterson: Sharp of you to be aware of that, Sam. You're right.

I've noticed in the last six weeks you've been consistently late. This isn't like your previous record. I think we should evaluate some of the things happening with you. Can you pinpoint why the tardiness, Sam?

Sam: Yes, Mr. Peterson, I think I can. I'll level with you. I'm pretty bored with the job I'm doing now. I've tried to adjust to the routine of the "cage," but it's gotten to me to the point where I don't really look forward to getting here in the morning. I guess I find a way subconsciously to be late, just about every day.

Mr. Peterson: Well, Sam, at least we know what's causing this situation. I wish you'd have come to me about it before this. Now that we know what's happening with you, let's see where you think you could be better satisfied in our organization.

Let's start with you putting down some ideas of what job you'd like to have. Outline a job description for me. Then, we'll go over it together and get Sam squared away so he'll *want* to come to work in the morning.

EVALUATION

Passivity doesn't locate problems. Involvement does! This case demonstrates the need to be less passive to get to the real problem. We need to level to have understanding. There's a need to share thinking. This can be done, however, only when the initial passivity is overcome. Once Mr. Peterson and Sam began talking and sharing thinking, the real problem surfaced.

The most important step in overcoming passivity is involvement —real involvement in everyday living. In our relations with other human beings, we tend toward friction. None of us is immune from making mistakes with other people. We're bound to encounter hurts from others. When we do, rather than withdraw like the turtle into its solitary house, we should face the situation, clear it up! Go onward! Avoid passivity!

EMPLOY DIRECTNESS

Thoreau says, "Our lives are frittered away by detail—specify, specify!" Much of our conversation is laden with an overabundance of wording, words that aren't to the point of the subject. This can cause a jamming of the listening mechanism. When the speaker isn't direct, the listener isn't always sure of his point. If you want to confuse your listener, just be nondirective. You've got him! He won't even know the name of the ball game.

A manager must be direct to insure understanding. When addressing someone in conversation, be specific in stating the purpose of your dialogue. *Don't speak in generalities.* State what it is you want to explore—a specific topic. This creates a friendly atmosphere of frankness when dealing with people and their problems.

The dialogist develops a high degree of credibility for himself by employing directness. Beating around the bush indicates a lack of self-assurance, personal conviction in self or product, indecision, reluctance to discuss an issue, and a lack of preparation. If we aren't direct (clear and plain) in our dealings, it's easy to misunderstand and to be misunderstood.

Levels of directness

There are levels of directness whereby we get our message across either quickly, or not at all. The following statements are all directed toward obtaining the Smith report. Each will produce action in varying degrees, depending on the level of directness employed.

Fourth level: "What are you doing?" (Least action)

Third level: "Wonder where the Smith report is?" (Eventual action)

Second level: "Do you have the Smith report?" (Possible action)

First level: "Would you get the Smith report for me, please?" (Action)

The first level should produce the Smith report for the speaker; he's *asking* for the Smith report. On the second level, if the other person had the Smith report he might have given it to the speaker. However, the second level wasn't a direct request. Levels three and four were such vague questions, they would have commanded action only with additional discussion. Being specific—direct—we can get the job done more efficiently, more quickly.

Instead of beating around the bush asking for something or asking for help, *ask for it!* (*Note:* It's suggested to *ask* for help, not to *tell* someone to help you.) Allow the other person to participate. Suggest that you have a need and would appreciate his help in working toward a solution. Define your problem (need), and ask his thinking on solving it or resolving it. *Ask* his opinion. As a manager you're more apt to get support and cooperation this way. *Employ the first level of directness for the first line of action.*

Why aren't we direct?

Why do people fail to employ directness? Often we fail to think about what we want to say until we start talking. Result: We have to organize as we go along. If we take time to organize in advance, we can save time when we get to the presentation of our ideas. Organization helps us to obtain a specific result. We'll know what we want to say, to whom we want to say it, and how we want to say it.

We fail to employ directness because we don't want to hurt someone, yet *we can hurt more because we don't face the issue.* If something is bugging you, say so, even though it may hurt the other person and in turn hurt you. At least then you'll know what the score really is. Even when someone lashes out at you, you may be hurt but you can say, "Thank you for telling me where I really stand. Now, let's see what I can do to change things." Through directness you'll arrive at a point of departure and can go from there.

When people hedge around, it's difficult to know the true meaning of what's being said. Hedging can so dilute the meaning, the real issues aren't heard or aren't believed. Case in point is *Slay the Dragon!*—

Case Study No. 15 / Slay the Dragon!

Cy Collier is a new divisional sales manager for a large cement company. Cy's having a problem with one of his salesmen, Bert Taylor. He isn't meeting the sales volume Cy feels should be coming out of his territory. Cy's conclusion is, he has to fire Bert, no matter what. The "no matter what" involves the fact that Bert has a wife and five children. He's paying on a home and car, etc. Nonetheless business is business, and Cy has made his decision.

He meets Bert in his territory. They have dinner after having made several calls together in the afternoon. The conversation goes like this:

Bert: That last customer sure is a tough one. I've called on him, I don't know how many times. He never seems to have time to see me.

Cy: Why don't you call before you go to see him?

Bert: Oh, I've tried that, too. It still doesn't seem to do any good. One day, I had an appointment to see him. Three hours later, he said he was sorry but so many things had come up he wouldn't have time to see me that afternoon.

Cy: It sounds like you shouldn't have stayed all that time, anyway. Didn't you have any other calls to make that afternoon?

Bert: Yes, but they were friends. I called them and told them I'd been delayed and couldn't get there that afternoon.

Cy: These things are tough to deal with I know, Bert. How do you feel you're doing with your territory? Do you think it's too big for you?

Bert: Oh, no. I like the size, and my customers. They're fine folks, and outside of little frustrations like this guy today, I like the people I work with.

Cy: Do you think you might be happier in something else, like working at some business other than sales?

Bert: Oh, no. I've been a salesman all of my life. You know how that is—once a salesman, always a salesman.

Cy: That's just my point, Bert. Maybe you weren't cut out to be in sales in the first place.

Bert: Hell, I don't know what I'd do other than this. I may not be a hot-shot salesman, but I do all right. I'm making it.

Cy: I'm not so sure about that, Bert. I have my doubts you're making it as good as you should be. I think we should be getting twice the volume out of this territory.

Bert: Maybe some other guy could sell more, but I offer my customers service and friendship. That keeps up a good company image for us. I think that's important, too.

Cy: Of course company image is important, but we can't make profit on just that. We've got to have sales. Yours just aren't coming up to what they should. I've watched you operate. I think you'd be better off in something besides the cement business if you want to stay in sales.

Bert: Cy, I've been with this company so long, I don't know anything else. No, I think the cement industry is growing. I want to stay with it.

Cy: If you want to stay with it, Bert, it's going to have to be with some other company. I can't justify keeping you on the payroll with your record looking the way it is. I wish it were otherwise, but I can't see it.

Bert: Well, there's always tomorrow, Cy. Maybe things haven't been too good for me recently. With the wife and five kids, I've had things kinda rough. I've had to take a little time with them away from business.

Cy: I understand your problems, Bert, and believe me, I wish there were something I could do to help you out. But, my hands are tied. There's nothing I can do to help you. I have to think of the company first.

Bert: Sure you do. And I'm going to put the company first, too. I realize I've got more I can do to activate business. I'm going to really get in there and pitch!

Cy: I just can't take that chance any more, Bert. You've been a good guy, and I like you and your wife and the kids. But I have to think of the company. I just can't let it go on like this.

Bert: Well, we'll see. I gotta go now. It's the kids bedtime. They always want me to be home to tuck 'em in. But, thanks, Cy, for the talk. You're a real buddy.

Cy: Good night, Bert. And tell your wife I'm sorry, too.

Bert: You bet. Good night.

Cy and Bert parted. Cy went to his motel, upset by having to let Bert go. With genuine understanding of Bert's obligations, he really hated to fire him. In fact, Cy's conscience bothered him about his action, yet he knew his first loyalty had to be the company. Nevertheless, he spent a sleepless night with concern about what he'd had to do.

Next morning, bright and early at 7:45 A.M. a brisk knock came at Cy's motel door. Wearily he opened it. There, bathed in the brilliant sunshine, stood Bert, toothpaste smile gleaming.

Bert: Morning, Cy. All ready to go out there and slay the dragons?

Cy: (Sleepily) What the hell to you mean, slay the dragons?

Bert: I'm full of energy and ready to go to work!

Cy: You idiot, didn't you hear me last night? I fired you!

Bert: Oh, come on, Cy, quit kidding. Go ahead and get dressed. I'll meet you in the coffee shop.

PROBLEM

Cy still had Bert on the payroll because he'd failed to be direct with him. When an operation has to be done, it's less painful if the cut is made quickly.

ALTERNATE APPROACH

After the last call, Cy suggests that he and Bert have a cup of coffee. They're seated at a table in a coffee shop.

Bert: That last customer sure is a tough one. I've called on him, I don't know how many time. He never seems to have time to see me.

Cy: There's one in every territory, Bert. (Pause) I've been going over your records for the past couple of years. I've compared your production record with what the projected volume sales are for your territory. Bert, you haven't come near it. There's no way to soften something like this. We have to let you go. I've given the matter lots of consideration. When I talked it over with the area manager we agreed. We have to replace you here.

Bert: I don't think I'm hearing right, Cy. You mean I'm fired?

Cy: In essence, yes. You'll get severance pay, though. That'll give you something to go on. However I can help you, I'll be glad to.

Bert: But what about all my bills, and the wife and kids?

Cy: That's the purpose of severance, Bert. It'll help keep you going until you find something else. I regret this.

Bert: Damn, I had no idea.

Cy: It's my thinking, Bert, it may be better for you, too. You're capable of producing more and maybe with another company or another line, or even out of sales, you can make more money. You'll get your severance together with your current expenses and commissions. Let me know if I can do anything for you.

Bert: Maybe you're right, Cy. Maybe I can do better in something else. I don't know what the hell it'd be right now, but I'll start looking. Thanks for telling me straight.

EVALUATION

Cy stated his position and Bert knows he's released. There's no doubt in his mind about this because Cy was direct!

It's possible the manager does a favor when he discharges an unproductive employee. He does the company a favor obviously when a man isn't cutting his quota. He does the employee a favor because it's possible he'll be able to earn more in some other area, under different circumstances, or with a different product. Deadwood doesn't help the tree to grow—better remove it.

Rules of directness

1. Address yourself to the proper person(s). Get to the person who has the authority to do the job, to say "yes" or "no," to bring action to your cause.

2. Know the purpose of your verbalization. Is it to inform, explain, instruct, clarify, decide? State the purpose; don't keep people guessing.

3. Make a clear statement of what your demands and expectations are, the rational basis for goals, and realistic ways for the other person to meet these demands. Specify precisely what's at stake, how the changes you seek will benefit both sides.

As the following case illustrates, state clearly what course of action is to be taken and what results you expect.

Case Study No. 16 / Oh, God, Help Me, Please!

Ken Williams is a maintenance engineer in a boiler-manufacturing plant. He's a veteran of the Korean War, and a six-year employee of this company. His immediate superior is Stan Adams, a sturdy, reliable, competent manager. Stan calls Ken into his office.

Stan: It's been awhile, Ken, since we've reviewed your job performance. Today might be a good time to do this.

Ken: (Obviously upset and suspicious) So, what's wrong?

Stan: I'm not aware that anything's wrong. Is there something I should know about? *Is* there something wrong?

Ken: You're bugging me. There's nothing wrong with me!

Stan: Who said there was? You're hard to get along with any more and I think I know why.

Ken: You do? Now, just what would you think is wrong with me?

Stan: I think you're hooked on heroin!

Ken: The hell you say! And so, what if I am?

Stan: You admit it! I knew I was right. There's nothing I can say, Ken, except we can't keep you. As of right now, you're through.

Ken: That's it?

Stan: That's it! We can't have an addict working here!

PROBLEM

Stan was too direct with Ken. Because of his suspicions, he was ready to take what Ken implied as an admission. However, Ken didn't admit being a drug user. He merely asked, "And so, what if I am?" Ken gave Stan no basis for his assumptions. Stan didn't allow Ken to give his thinking, he didn't attempt working toward any solution with Ken, he merely dismissed him. It's a costly turnover to dismiss an engineer (or any employee) unnecessarily. What should management's stand be on drug use? How should the problem be handled?

ALTERNATE APPROACH

Stan: It's been awhile, Ken, since we've reviewed your job performance. Today might be a good time to do this.

Ken: (Obviously upset and suspicious) So, what's wrong?

Stan: Wrong?

Ken: You must have called this meeting for something.

Stan: It's just routine, Ken. But I hear a lot of defensiveness in what you're saying. Can you tell me why you're upset?

Ken: I don't like being intimidated this way.

Stan: Intimidated?

Ken: Yes! Everybody's watching me lately. Especially you!

Stan: You feel people are watching you for no reason.

Ken: Yes, they're watching me and it makes me nervous. I can't concentrate.

Stan: You feel people are interfering with your performance.

Ken: I keep making mistakes because they're watching me. I don't like to get slowed down and feel intimidated.

Stan: I've noticed you've been a little jumpy recently, Ken. Your behavior in general seems to have changed. Can you tell me why you were asleep in the storage room this morning?

Ken: I don't know. I just got sleepy, and I guess I fell asleep! Is there anything wrong with that?

Stan: Yes, Ken, there is something wrong with it. It's a dangerous thing to have you drowsy and sleepy and slow on the trigger. It's a safety hazard to you and other workers. You weren't this way until a few months ago. Can you tell me why you think your behavior has changed this way?

Ken: No.

Stan: Will you have a physical, Ken? We'll try to uncover your problem.

Ken: You just want to do a urine test on me! You know damned well what'll show up! You know damned well what's wrong with me! I'm shooting up and it's getting worse. I have a habit that's gotten to the point I can't function without heavy fixes. God, what can I do? I don't want to go on like this. I don't want to! I'm high on heroin most of the time. I don't want to cause an accident! My life at home is hell and it's no better here. Oh, God, help me! Please!

Stan: We'll get help for you, Ken. If you really mean it, that you don't want to go on this way, there are treatment centers available for you. We can get you on a withdrawal program and start you toward rehabilitation. We want to help you and to keep you on here, Ken, but your behavior has to change.

Ken: This damned monkey has me and I've gotta kick it! Help me! I'll do anything!

Stan: You'll have to detoxify and go on rehabilitation. I have no idea how long this'll take for you, Ken. If you'll stick with it, I'll do my best to help you and keep your job available. If you don't stay on the rehabilitation, Ken, I have to tell you now you'll be fired!

Ken: Let's get started with this thing. I want to! God, I want to!

EVALUATION

Stan recognized the behavior changes in Ken. He directed his remarks toward the behavior, not toward Ken. He attacked the problem, not the person. He concentrated on the safety hazard involved in Ken's behavior.

Having substantiated his evaluation of the changes in Ken's behavior, Stan is direct in asking Ken to submit to a physical, yet he doesn't ask specifically for a urinalysis. This is a tip-off to a drug user that you suspect him. Also, if this weren't a case of drug addiction, Stan hadn't falsely accused Ken by asking for just the urine test.

OBSERVATION

Drug abuse is a recognized problem in business and industry today. *It isn't on the decrease.* Therefore, it's imperative that the manager knows (a) its symptoms, (b) what stand *his company* takes on the problem of drug abuse, and (c) what treatment is available locally. Drug abuse is often a difficult thing to detect, and its treatment and handling are still in experimental stages.

What should be management's stand on the drug problem? Graham S. Finney, Commissioner of the Addition Services Agency of the City of New York, states:

> Drug abuse is a growing manifestation in industry and it is the wise manager who recognizes that the problem can neither be tucked under a convenient rug nor solved by means of discharge. Responsibility to top management, as well as to the employees themselves, would dictate the establishment of procedures whereby employees discovered abusing drugs or voluntarily furnishing this information could be referred to drug treatment programs operating in the locality for rehabilitation and, hopefully, eventual restoration to a productive and responsible life. And, along the same path, management has an obligation to give a rehabilitated ex-addict opportunity for employment without penalties for his past life.

Maslow says, "Everyone is to be informed as completely as possible i.e.: everything relevant to the situation . . . People need to know, knowing is good for them, the truth, the facts, and honesty tend to be curative, healing, to taste good, to be familiar, etc."[12]

4. Learn to punctuate! When people get too much information, they forget most of what's been said. Too much information jams the listening mechanism, and this becomes no communication at all. People can concentrate on only one thing at a time. Your listeners' attention will be held when what you have to say is meaningful to them. State your case succinctly, then *stop!* We have a human tendency to overelaborate, to exaggerate, to magnify, expecially when we are in a highly emotional state. Instead of strengthening our position, we're apt to weaken it by overamplification. This can cloud rather than clarify.

5. Avoid digression. If we don't want to face an issue, we'll probably digress. Or, if we want to change the subject, we'll digress. Or, if we're unsure what we want to say, we'll digress. Any of these reasons is no reason for digression. We should introduce only material that has to do with the point in question, that contributes to understanding a particular point at issue.

6. Put forth one idea at a time! Even while focusing on your words, the listener has to digest one idea before he can take in the

next idea. Executives have a tendency to crowd all their messages into one speech. *Be brief, factual, direct!* We can take a lesson from advertising and commercials to concentrate on one product one point at a time. Otherwise, people don't know what's being sold. Put forth only one concept at a time. Be sure that one concept is understood before setting forth another.

7. Present material in order—chronologically; as a sequence of events; according to importance; alphabetically, etc. Retention of information is made easier, and it's easier, too, for the listener to grasp true meanings when information is presented in this manner.

8. Talk in the other person's language. Technical terms, complicated statistics, involved details of ideas beyond the pertinent subject area, all may prove intelligence, but they suffice to tune out the listener. Speak in their terms at their level of interest. Direct your conversation to their needs and goals. Be specific! Be direct in your language. You aren't out to prove your word-power knowledge, but out to get through to the other person.

9. For the manager, keeping conversation objective will help keep it direct. When you become subjective, there's a tendency to introduce irrelevancies into the dialogue. Objectivity produces a more rational evaluation of facts rather than personal feelings.

10. Stay on target by getting feedback and giving it. Feedback is the steering apparatus for keeping dialogue on a direct path toward an established goal.

Negative action of directness

There are some undesirable elements in being *too* direct in an approach:

1. *Fragmentation:* One of these elements is fragmentation. Let's note the differences in these two statements:

(a) "Your reports are incomplete. Be more specific."

(b) "Your reports have been on time regularly, Pete, and I appreciate this. I need to go over them with you, though. I see there's some information on items 2 and 4 that I need to know more about."

The first of these statements was fragmented. Although it's direct, it doesn't tell the person what's wrong with the reports. The only suggestion for any avenue of improvement was the generalized advice, "be specific." Specific about what?

The second statement tells what items are incomplete. It suggests an avenue of correction—to talk it over. Make it a rule to offer *direct, specific* criticism when leveling with someone. In addition, ask for or offer an avenue for change. In this way your leveling has told the person specifically what's wrong and has suggested a way in which it may be changed.

2. *Absolutes:* Dealing in absolutes can be an offensive form of directness. Listeners can turn quickly from such words as always, all, and never. They can be too direct when they're used to say, "You're *always* late" . . . "*All* I ever hear about your work is complaints" . . . "You *never* turn in a report on time." Although it may be reasonably true that these absolutes apply, using them is a psychological hazard. It implies the recipient has *never* done *anything* right, he's *always* wrong, and *all* of his future he'll be a dud in your eyes! He hasn't a chance to change. Because they're absolutes, these are treacherous forms of directness. Absolutes are direct, but threatening. They carry the weight of undisputed authority. Absolutes can squelch creativity and response. If we think in this way, it'll help us avoid using absolutes: *Things are neither wrong nor right—they're effective or ineffective.*

3. *Threats:* Threats are direct, but they can lose the cause for the speaker. Threats are difficult to deal with. They automatically produce hostility and defensiveness in the receiver. They're the action of a parent-child relationship that is demeaning to a thinking person. The result may be total rejection or an attitude of "Just you try it, you bastard, just you try!" Beating a person down guarantees neither agreement nor submission. To the contrary, it's apt to activate antagonism and rejection. It attacks the intellect and ego of the other person, but it doesn't change his thinking to accord with yours. High-pressure techniques and scare-tactics, together with threats, turn people off!

4. *Tact:* Any approach that isn't tactful (within reason) stands a chance of producing negative responses in the other person. This doesn't imply we have to be saccharine-sweet! It does imply that it's indigenous to desirable dialogue to recognize the other person as a human being and treat him as such. We can be direct, indeed, but let's garnish the directness with tact. *I Thought I'd Lived It Down* is an example of this point:

Case Study No. 17 / I Thought I'd Lived It Down

For bonding purposes the personnel manager of an organization was checking old employees' records. The file of Daniel Adams, a nine-year employee, divulged his arrest fourteen years before. As a result of the arrest he had served one year in the reformatory. The personnel manager brought this to the attention of Mel Randal, Daniel's supervisor. Mel has called Daniel to his office.

Mel: Hello, Daniel. Sit down.

Daniel: Thank you, Mel.

Mel: There's something I have to tell you, Daniel. At the request of several of the management group, I've been asked to notify you we're terminating your employment, effective immediately.

Daniel: I don't understand.

Mel: Your arrest record has been discovered. We can no longer consider you in our employ.

Daniel: Just like that?

Mel: Just like that.

Daniel: What can I say?

Mel: There's nothing to say, Daniel. You understand, we can't keep you on here. It just isn't possible.

PROBLEM

Mel employed directness, but as a result he may have lost an employee worth keeping. He failed to talk the situation out with Daniel, or to give him any options. *Tact* is still necessary in a personal emotional situation such as this.

ALTERNATE APPROACH

Mel: Hello, Daniel. Sit down.

Daniel: Thank you, Mel.

Mel: I've been looking over your record with us here, Daniel. You've been an acceptable, reliable employee. You've made some good creative suggestions that have benefited the company.

Daniel: I've enjoyed working here. I like my work and the people I work with.

Mel: Something else has appeared on your record. I find there was an arrest charge filed against you fourteen years ago. You were convicted and served a year in the state reformatory.

Daniel: It's finally come out! God knows I've tried to hide that. I thought I'd lived it down!

Mel: In my book, Daniel, you're a good employee—above average. *I* have no bone to pick with you. It isn't just the charge and arrest that bothers us; the fact is, the charge was for homosexuality. Somehow, regrettably, this information has gotten on the grapevine. There are several people who know about it. What are your feelings about this?

Daniel: They're mixed, Mel. I'm shocked that all this has come out. I resent it having leaked to the grapevine. My personal life has nothing to do with my business life. I feel I'm being fired, but I don't want to leave—I just don't know.

Mel: My reaction is, I don't give a damn what you do with your personal life as long as it doesn't interfere with your business life. But, I also feel it's only fair to tell you what I know about this. Some of management is a bit uptight about it. I think I can handle them. I'd say that the decision is yours to make.

Daniel: What you're saying is, you personally have no gripe with this happening of the past; some of management might object, but you think you can handle them. Then it seems the problem lies between me and the employees who know about my gay activities. Do I think I can face them? Work with them? Do I *want* to work with them knowing that they *do* or *might* know the story? That's a hell of a decision to have to make. I don't think I can make it this quickly, Mel.

Mel: Understandable, Daniel. Why don't we do this? Take your time. Let's give it a week and talk it over again next Wednesday at ten thirty. Meanwhile, if you come to a decision before then, you know my number—just call. If there's anything else you'd like to talk about—just call.

Daniel: All I can say is, thanks! You've been considerate of my feelings. I appreciate that. I respect your awkward position. I don't want to make it tough on you.

Mel: Don't worry about me. The thing you have to consider is, whether you want to resign or stay. The decision is up to you. However you want to deal with it, I'll go along with your conclusion.

Daniel: Thanks, Mel, for your candor. I'd rather know what the situation really is. I can deal with it better having all of the facts. Now I've got to do some thinking. I'll see you next week.

EVALUATION

Although we don't know what Daniel will do, we know Mel handled this in a more tactful and intelligent way.

Knowing the facts, Daniel will be able to come to a more stable conclusion. Had any of these elements been withheld from him, they could cause confusion later. By possession of these facts, Daniel is better equipped to make his decision.

In talking with Bob Milne, president of the Mattachine Society of New York City, the oldest and largest of some six hundred homosexual groups throughout the United States, Mr. Milne suggests that the laws differ from state to state governing the legal stand that employers might take regarding gay sex. These laws are constantly changing. It therefore behooves an employer to know the local laws before contemplating dismissing a person on homosexual charges. According to Mr. Milne, the stand of the Mattachine Society and other such groups is: If a person is a reliable employee who performs his job acceptably, he should be allowed to pursue his personal life as he chooses so long as it does not interfere with his capabilities on the job.

Difficult issues need to be handled with directness and dignity. The element of dignity helps them to be more palatably received.

5. *Oratorical:* When an oratorical technique of delivery is used in one-to-one conversation, it can destroy the sincerity and credibility of both subject matter and speaker. Although it's a direct form of delivery, an oratorical monologue comes off sounding like a canned spiel and is easily tuned out by the listener. The too-well-pronounced word, overarticulation, perfect syntax, the sixty-four-dollar words, lack of slang and/or contractions—all take away from the sincerity, believability, and honesty of interpersonal communications.

6. *Et cetera:* Etcetera's are the enrichment factors of a speech. They are analogy, caricature, slogans, quotations, and parables. The etceteras of speeches must be used sparingly in one-to-one communications or directions will be destroyed. They are more meaningful in professional speeches. In conversation they can destroy directness and cloud the issues.

Learn to engage in using the first level of directness. It accomplishes your goal more quickly. Send out your message clearly on the receiver's wavelength. Direct your words on the level of the receiver's needs and goals. Be concise in your delivery without being brusque. Obtain and give feedback for clarification and verification. This lets you know you're on a direct beam headed toward your desired goal of understanding and problem solving.

RESPECT FEELINGS

Recognize and respect feelings

What are feelings? Feelings are the internal emotional factors controlling our thinking and our actions. It's important that we learn to recognize feelings in others, to understand what they're *really* thinking, why they respond as they do, what their real problems are. Feelings influence what we say, how we react to certain stimuli, why we profess particular attitudes. True, a manager needs to watch for *facts* presented in dialogue, but he must also watch for *feelings*. He should probe for feelings, encouraging their expression. In this way he's better equipped to understand his associates and his employees.

The Managerial Grid (Blake and Mouton) refers to the manager's concern for production *and his concern for people.*[13] By hitting a high balance of these two elements, the manager is better able to accomplish his goals. *The Managerial Grid* indicates concern for production *and* concern for people are necessary elements of a manager's attitudes, and indeed, complement each other to achieve work objectives. The optimum rating on Blake's Grid is 9-9, scoring nine points on concern for production and nine points on concern for people. In order to achieve this ratio, it appears one prerequisite would be for the manager to understand people better by engaging them in dialogue, respecting their feelings and needs.

How does the manager respect an employee's needs and feelings? He attempts:

1. to see anyone with whom he's speaking as a co-worker, on a common problem;
2. to treat the co-worker as an equal human being;
3. to follow the worker's line of thought;

4. to share the attitudes and ideas of the worker with understanding; and

5. to express a genuine interest in what the person has to say.

Why a manager's concern for feelings?

Why is a manager concerned about the feelings of his people? Because emotions and feelings affect job performance. There can be a direct relationship between emotions and production. According to Schmidt and Tannenbaum:

> Repression (of feelings) almost always costs something. If, indeed, the differences are important to the persons involved, their feelings may come to be expressed indirectly, in ways that could reduce productivity. Every manager has witnessed situations in which ideas are resisted, not on the basis of their merit, but on the basis of who advocated them. Or he has seen strong criticism arising over mistakes made by a particularly disliked individual.
>
> Much has been said and written about "hidden agenda." People may discuss one subject, but the *way* they discuss it and the positions they take with respect to it may actually be determined by factors lying beneath the surface of the discussion. Hidden agenda are likely to abound in an atmosphere of repression.
>
> When strong feelings are involved in unexpressed differences, the blocking of these feelings creates frustration and hostility which may be misdirected toward "safe" targets. Differences, and the feelings generated by them, do not ordinarily disappear by being ignored. They fester beneath the surface and emerge at inopportune moments to create problems for the manager and his organization.[14]

Feelings and emotions can disable one's production capabilities as can a physical disorder. The big problem is detecting emotional strain. A physical malfunction (i.e., a broken leg) may manifest itself more noticeably and be more readily recognized than the emotional, which conceals itself from early detection.

When someone suffers chronic fatigue from strain of anxiety and emotional tension, he isn't able to produce at peak rate. Someone suffering insomnia from worry is sleepy on the job. His production rate is bound to decrease, as is his efficiency.

The same sleepy or tired worker is a safety risk. He isn't alert in his physical reactions on the job, whether it's driving a car, fork lift, or crane. The emotionally upset laborer is a safety hazard when he isn't concentrating on the job at hand but is dwelling on other matters preying on his mind. Safety requires attention to the immediate task, not to problems "out there."

What about the manager or supervisor himself? Do his feelings and emotions have bearing on his subordinates? Yes, *feelings and emotions are contagious, especially in the person who is the catalyst.* The manager can set the tone for his employees with what he's feeling. Can emotions be concealed?—Not for long. It isn't easy to hide intense emotions. They can be glossed over somewhat, but not indefinitely—surely not with personnel you're contacting on a daily basis. Therefore, it's important for the manager to be able to recognize feelings and emotions within himself, and to deal with them before they spill over to his employees.

There's another reason the manager should be aware of feelings and emotions. If he detects something amiss in an employee, he can confront the person about the problem in an attempt to help the latter understand it. If necessary, he can refer the employee to the medical department or for counseling before the emotions precipitate a crisis endangering the safety of the individual and/or his co-workers.

Erupting emotions can cause other problems for the manager. They stifle creativity, diminish personal relationships, distract concentration, irritate others, nurture dissatisfaction, encourage transfer, and increase turnover. Recognizing emotions and feelings is a vital part of a manager's responsibility. Once he has recognized them, the manager must learn to deal with them in himself and in others.

"Feelings" words

How do we recognize feelings? We recognize them by body English, expressions, gestures, tone of voice, pitch, and by words themselves. The words that tell us about feelings and are called "feelings words." They can display *real* meaning. When we know how to listen for them, we're better equipped to uncover what's beneath feelings words. The following is a list of words that are typical tip-off words for the listener. Generally they are preceded by "I feel ——," or "I'm ——."

disgusted	frustrated	repressed
angry	left out	uptight
afraid	vindictive	inadequate
helpless	irritated	sick
depressed	resentment	oppressed
numb	bitterness	cheated
hostile	rejection	hurt
turned off	overlooked	lonely
restless	teed off	stymied
stupid	embarrassed	incompetent

When these words or others like them appear in dialogue, they're indicators for the manager to ask questions to uncover what they mean to the other person. (Remember, the same word can mean different things to different people.) Often, this is the only way to focus on the *real* problem.

If an employee says, "I feel cheated," your response might be, "What do you mean, cheated?"

When your peer says, "I've been depressed recently," you might reply, "What seems to be causing your depression?"

When someone says, "I'm shocked," you could reply, "You're shocked. What shocks you?"

In the above sentences the adjective was the key word to pinpoint the feelings. *Listen for the adjective, feed it back for clarification, for amplification. The adjective often is the arrow pointing to feelings.*

When feelings words yield an expression about what is really going on inside another person, you must respect the exposure of this inner self.

Respecting feelings

Each person has a right to exist. Therefore, there must be mutual respect of a person's feelings. What is respect? As Erich Fromm, psychoanalyst, describes it, "Respect is not fear and awe; it denotes, in accordance with the root of the word (*respicere*-to look at), the ability to see a person as he is, to be aware of his unique individuality."[15]

Conflict occurs where rights are being infringed on by someone else. You have the prerogative to set limits when your rights are transgressed. In the case of *The Colossal Copout*, we'll see what happens when the rights of Leo and Dave aren't respected:

Case Study No. 18 / The Colossal Copout

Two research engineers, Dave Procter and Leo Russell, have been assigned to work on a project that will see fruition in several years. They're top men in this area, working diligently toward completion of the new project. However, when bonus time came at the end of the year neither Dave nor Leo got a bonus. Several other engineers with less seniority got bonuses for projects that had been implemented during the year. Dave and Leo decide to confront their supervisor, Ben Dailey, about this matter.

Ben: Come in, Dave, Leo. From the tone of your memo, you seem disturbed about something.

Dave and Leo: We are!

Dave: Go ahead, Leo, tell him what we're about.

Leo: Ben, as you know, Dave and I are assigned to do a forecast project in research. When we took the assignment, we knew it'd be a few years before our findings would be implemented. We've worked damned hard all this year on the project. We show good results for the time we've spent——

Leo: (interrupting while erupting) That's what bugs us, Ben. We've given our all for this project. Yet, when the bonus bag was opened this year, there was nothing in it for us.

Dave: You're damned right! Who got the bonuses? Several guys who've been here a shorter time and who've done less important work. Why? What happened?

Ben: It's company policy! That's what happened.

Dave: What the hell do you mean, company policy? We're dedicated men, we're loyal, we're productive, yet——

Ben: (interrupting) There really isn't anything to be said or considered. You know what company policy is: A bonus for implemented ideas, that's company policy. I have to stand by it.

Leo: Well, Ben, if you have to stand by *that*, stand by it alone. As far as I'm concerned, consider my resignation effective right now.

Dave: I can't believe what I hear, Ben. If you're sure you have to stand by an archaic policy like that—or maybe you're hiding behind the apron strings of that colossal copout, "It's company policy"

—whatever it is, I feel like Leo. Count me out. May as well make my resignation effective today, too.

Ben: That's your decision? Then I have to abide by it in the same way I have to abide by company policy. I'll have your checks drawn up. We'll terminate your employment effective now.

PROBLEM

Ben's failure to respect the feelings of Leo and Dave and his failure to communicate with them to their satisfaction.

Ben's failure to respect feelings effects an impasse for Leo and Dave. Ben paralyzed communications with his statement, "It's against company policy." This is the great dialogue shut-off. It's difficult to top that statement.

ALTERNATE APPROACH

Ben: Come in Dave, Leo. Your memo indicated you're pretty disturbed about something.

Dave and Leo: We are!

Dave: Go ahead, Leo, tell him what we're about.

Leo: Ben, as you know, Dave and I are assigned to do a forecast project in research. When we took the assignment, we knew it'd be a few years before our findings would be implemented. We've worked damned hard all this year on the project. We show good results for the time we've spent——

Ben: I hear lots of frustration in what you're saying, Leo. I know you've worked hard. How do you feel about this, Dave?

Dave: I feel the same way, but you haven't hard our *real* gripe, Ben. We're uptight about the bonus envelopes. When they were passed out, we were passed by! There were lots of guys who haven't been here as long as we have, who haven't produced as much as we have, who got the bonus checks. Why?

Ben: Well, that's company policy, to pay a bonus for ideas implemented during the year. These fellows came up with things that took shape and were used this past year.

Dave: And you call that fair? That's plainly some archaic law that's still hanging in there and affecting us. What can we do to get it changed, or make some sort of amendment to it, Ben?

Ben: I'm not sure what can be done, Dave. Do I read you right?

What you're saying is you want some bonus compensation for your efforts although they haven't been implemented yet?

Dave: You're damned right, Ben. That's exactly what I mean.

Leo: We took this assignment knowing it'd be a couple of years before it's completed. But we sure didn't expect you'd hold to that old chestnut of company policy! We feel there should be a form of bonus payment to include engineers working on long-range projects.

Ben: I hear both of you loud and clear! I recognize your feelings and your frustration. I'll say this: I'll expose this to the proper people at a meeting early next week. You can be sure I'll present your side as you've given it to me. Or, would you like to attend the session?

Leo: Not necessarily, Ben. As far as I'm concerned, you can represent me.

Dave: Me too, Ben. You know what we're saying. We like the company. We want to do our best for company objectives. We feel there are times when the twig must bend to meet unusual circumstances. Right now, Leo and I are sorta unusual circumstances. We appreciate your understanding. We'll wait to hear the outcome of this meeting.

Leo: You're our ambassador. Let us know what happens.

EVALUATION

The cost of replacing Leo and Dave would have been high. By flexing, Ben may be able to save the high cost of turnover of two key men. Leo and Dave express what they feel would be a course of action that would allow them to continue with the company, with their feelings respected and their rights acknowledged. We must allow others their rights as individuals and respect these rights. Leo and Dave were telling Ben in essence: "We respect your right to feel the way you do about company policy, but we don't choose to work under it as it stands." In like instance, Ben told them, "I respect your right to disagree. I'll present your thinking to the right people and see what they'll do about it." Attitudes such as these are fertile ground for understanding and problem solving.

Joshua Liebman expresses it this way in *Peace of Mind:* "Tolerance (respect) is the positive and cordial effort to understand another's beliefs, practices, and habits without necessarily sharing or accepting them."[16]

According to Schmidt and Tannenbaum, in respecting feelings we respect the individual:

"The manager, recognizing and accepting feelings such as fear, jealousy, anger, or anxiety, may make it possible for the participants squarely to face their true feelings. The effective manager does not take a critical attitude toward these feelings by, in effect, saying, 'You have no right to feel angry!' Rather, he tries sincerely to communicate his sympathetic feelings.

"Ordinarily, we do no real service to people by encouraging a repression of their feelings or by criticizing them for experiencing fear, anger, and so forth. Such criticism—whether implied or expressed openly—may block the search for new ways out of the controversy."[17]

We don't talk down to the individual, we don't belittle him, or tell him he's stupid, or to forget about it. We give the other person the right to be hurt. It's human to feel hurt. Respect this right. Whatever is a problem for someone *is a problem for him.* It won't evaporate, it must be dealt with as we'll see in *It's the Little Things That Count:*

Case Study No. 19 / It's the Little Things That Count

Chester Rawlins is vice-president of engineering in a major production plant. He's been with the company eight years and has just had his office location changed. He's now in the executive area of the main building and has been in this location five days. His immediate superior, Hank Andrews, walks into Chester's spacious new office.

Hank: How goes it in your new office, Chester?

Chester: Great, Hank—in a way.

Hank: What do you mean, in a way?

Chester: I may as well tell you. I think I'm getting the old discrimination treatment.

Hank: Discrimination treatment?

Chester: Yes! Have you dialed my number since I moved here?

Hank: No, I guess I haven't.

Chester: Well, there's no zero in my number, and I resent it!

Hank: Oh, that's stupid, Chester—just because a zero is included in the top executives' numbers. With your move you lost your zero. That isn't discrimination. Forget it! Just swing with a common old number. You'll live through it.

PROBLEM

Hank isn't listening to the feelings Chester is feeding him. Obviously, it's important to Chester's ego to have that zero in his phone number. According to Herzberg, it's these small hygiene factors that can make a difference if they aren't attended to.[18]

ALTERNATE APPROACH

Hank: How goes it in your new office, Chester?

Chester: Great, Hank—in a way.

Hank: What do you mean, in a way?

Chester: I may as well tell you. I think I'm getting the old discrimination treatment.

Hank: Discrimination treatment?

Chester: Yes. Have you dialed my number since I moved here?

Hank: No, I guess I haven't.

Chester: Well, there's no zero in my number, and I resent it!

Hank: Oh? I wasn't aware that you didn't have the zero. I hear you saying this is important to you, Chester.

Chester: You bet it is! I've worked damned hard to reach this level of executive stature. Then they give me a number that could belong to anyone in the plant!

Hank: It has to be one of two things. It's either that there are no zero numbers available now or it's an oversight. It isn't something that can't be rectified.

Chester: I appreciate whatever you can do for me. I haven't even given my number out. I'm afraid people will think I've been demoted. The sooner you can attend to this, the better.

Hank: You're coming in loud and clear! I'll let you know what to expect in a few minutes. Glad you mentioned this to me, Chester. No use having you unhappy over a thing like this.

EVALUATION

Often the little things are the things that *do* count! Listening for feelings and respecting feelings are important ingredients in keeping things running smoothly. Chester's problem seemed an irrelevancy to Hank until he perceived the feelings Chester was having about it. Listen to irrelevancies; couched in them can be deeper problems. Frequently they're the facade for intense emotions and relevancies.

Be patient and listen to what's being said. Be courteous and avoid employing sarcasm. Avoid overexplanation (this can be misconstrued as the parent talking down to the child). Put yourself in the other's shoes, or as a Japanese proverb puts it, "Pinch yourself and know how others feel."

"If this were said to me, how would I feel?" This is a good question to ask yourself as you engage in dialogue. If you wouldn't like to hear, "Don't be stupid," then avoid saying it to someone else. If you'd react adversely to someone saying, "That's a lousy attitude to have, let's get with it," then avoid saying it to someone else. If an employee says, "I'm frustrated by my job," instead of responding, "Don't be dumb, you have a good job," pick up on the word "frustrated." That's a feelings word. Ask what they mean: "Frustrated by your job? What about your job frustrates you?"

Anything you think you wouldn't want said to you, just stand in the other's shoes, pinch yourself, and know how others feel. If the pinch hurts, avoid saying it. This will engender understanding and decontaminate dialogical pollution.

The following case study points up the need to recognize, respect, and deal with feelings and emotions:

Case Study No. 20 / BAWWWWWWWAH!

It's near the close of a frantically busy day for Mr. Walsh and his secretary, Ann Prentice. Mr. Walsh buzzes and Ann comes into his office.

Mr. Walsh: Ann, we're in a bind! I have to be out of the office most of tomorrow. These letters need to be done now for me to sign them before I leave. Let's get at it. First letter to Mr. Angus Black, Severin Steel Mills, Youngstown, Ohio. Dear Angus, from the report you gave me in your last letter, it seems a meeting is mandatory. I'll coordinate my schedule with yours——(Ann starts sniffing while taking dictation. Tears begin streaming down her cheeks. The faster Mr. Walsh dictates, the more freely the tears flow until finally she bursts out in heavy sobs and an audible *BAWWWWWWWAH!*)

Mr. Walsh: For God's sake, Ann, what's wrong?

Ann: I——I——I (unable to answer, she tears away, daubing her nose with a tissue).

Mr. Walsh: Come on now, Ann, quit the tears. We've got work to do! Stop it! Ann! (Mr. Walsh goes around to Ann and shakes her.) Ann, snap out of it! Do you hear me, quit crying! (Ann's tears become more intense, nearing hysteria. Mr. Walsh rushes to the door, opens it and *yells*.) Miss Harrison! Come in here and do something with Ann! Get her to the john or something, then come back and take this dictation. It's got to be typed this evening before I leave.

PROBLEM

What to do when a woman cries on the job? What causes the tears? What can be done to stop them? Mr. Walsh seems to have less concern for Ann and more concern for getting the letters finished.

ALTERNATE APPROACH

Mr. Walsh: (When Ann began sobbing, before she got to the *real* tears.) Ann, are you about to cry? (She breaks out into tears. Mr. Walsh says calmly and reassuringly) Ann, your tears tell me something's wrong. (Pause) I want to help you. (Pause) I can't help you until you stop crying and tell me what bothering you. (Pause) Here Ann, take this handkerchief. (Ann blows into the handkerchief) That's better. (Pause) I don't know what caused the tears, but if I can help you, I will. Can you tell me what's wrong, Ann?

Ann: Oh, yes, Mr. Walsh. You always do this, just at the close of the day. You call me to do a dozen letters for you, and you want them done, like yesterday! (Becoming emotional.)

Mr. Walsh: (stunned) Ann, I hear what you're saying! I hadn't realized I was doing this. Why didn't you tell me before?

Ann: I thought you'd realize it's virtually impossible to do all you ask! Plus that, I think it's downright selfish and inconsiderate on your part!

Mr. Walsh: Well, you're really leveling with me—you've let me have it full blast. I think I have to agree with you. It *is* selfish and inconsiderate of me. (Ann's tears are now subsided to an occasional sniff.)

Ann: I'm sorry, Mr. Walsh. I didn't mean to let go at you that way, but I just can't take it at the end of a busy day like this, and you throw all of this work at me. I'm so uptight, I have to cry.

Mr. Walsh: What you're telling me is I'm a big s.o.b.

Ann: You said it! And I agree! (Tears have stopped and a smile of relief comes over Ann's face.)

Mr. Walsh: Let me say this, Ann. I appreciate your telling me off. I needed it. It *has been* inconsiderate of me to do this *in the past.* I assure you, I'll attempt doing differently in the future. I'll try to *not* give you any letters after three thirty—only emergency things after that.

Ann: That would surely help. It's a terrible frustration to work under these pressures. I don't want to let you down, but when I get pushed against a solid wall of no time, then the tears flow. But I feel better now, better for having talked this out with you. Let me take your most important letters now. I'll do the best I can with them yet this afternoon.

Mr. Walsh: "Good-Ann," you're a jewel! Thanks for putting up with me. Ready? Where was I?

Ann: You said, "I'll coordinate my schedule with yours———."

EVALUATION

Mr. Walsh asked, and Ann gave! They should have a much better working relationship in the future. Reason?—He got behind the tears to the real problem. He lost a few minutes getting to the problem, but the payoff in Ann's future production should reward him amply.

Mr. Walsh was sensitive to the feelings going on in Ann. Instead of ignoring them, he was direct in mentioning them. When Ann began crying, Mr. Walsh didn't become emotional. He kept his cool. *Talking to her calmly, reassuring her of his support,* he helped dispel her emotional outburst. (Someone has to stay calm in a crisis.)

OBSERVATION

The following is a statement made by N. Jeanne Wertz, Executive Coordinator of RE:WOMEN, a New York based management/employer data and counseling service on the subject of women employees:

A flare-up, a strained working situation, and/or tears over a late-day dictation crisis, is one of the more common examples of the results of the communication gap existing between male boss and female secretary.

Responses from hundreds of secretaries in a variety of firms and industries across the country, in discussion groups and personal interviews, indicate late-day dictation to be a major problem. It is one that can be solved, by the same methods that other management problems are solved. First, analyze the real problem. Second, get all the facts (i.e., get her side of the story and evaluate if late-day dictation *is* a consistent pattern), and third, set up the solution that is both productive and considerate to each party.

What makes a woman cry? This is a question asked by many men. Women cry because they're frustrated by some incident or incidents. *Frustration is what makes women cry.* Other than from sadness or joy, their tears flow from frustration at not being able to accomplish a goal. A woman may say, "I only cry when I'm really mad." Her anger comes from frustration at being unable to attain a goal. Ann was frustrated because she couldn't accomplish the goal of getting Mr. Walsh's letters done on time. It was this feeling of being unable to acocmplish a goal that caused her anger, that caused her tears.

Men vent anger by socking a golf ball, punching a handball, or swearing. It's all right for a man to get angry at his boss and vent his frustration (behind the boss's back) saying, "That sonofabitch! He can't do that to me!" But society doesn't accept a woman saying "sonofabitch" so instead she cries.

There's a recent concept *It's acceptable and healthy for a man to cry.* A feature story by John Poppy in *Look Magazine*, July 9, 1968, was entitled, "It's OK to Cry in the Office." It was an article directed toward men. It's important to understand the cause of such volatile emotions, and let them go!

A calm, cool production manager *once* became emotional in front of his subordinates. He quickly apologized for the flare of his temper. One of the group said, "What's the matter? Are you afraid to let us know you're human?"

Regarding tears, this from *Oliver Twist:* Mr. Bumble expresses the thinking of Charles Dickens, "It opens the lungs, washes the countenance, exercises the eyes and softens down the temper. So cry away!"

The Achilles'-heel syndrome

History records Achilles as a Greek warrior whose vulnerable point was his heel. All of us have an emotional Achilles' heel. It's that unprotected point in our emotional fiber that, when hit, is like an exposed nerve—we feel it! This point differs with different people. It may be fear of rejection, or we're "touchy" about being reminded of an error in judgment we've made at some previous time. We may dislike being kidded about being of a specific ethnic background, or that we're parsimonious in our dealings. We may be sensitive about discussing our personal relations or social activities. Whatever the particular area of vulnerability, we have it. When others know about it, it's cruel of them to use this as a weapon against us.

Let's assume that Charlie's Achilles' heel is his fear of rejection. His associates and manager know this. One day Charlie gains disfavor among his group. They decide to omit him from their luncheons and coffee breaks. They exclude him from decision making. They're rejecting him. They're kicking Charlie's Achilles' heel! His manager may decide to use this vulnerable point in a disciplinary manner. He withholds praise from Charlie. He doesn't dialogue with him regarding matters they would normally discuss. He's rejecting Charlie as a parent disciplining a child. The manager, too, has kicked Charlie's Achilles' heel. It would be better if Charlie's friends and manager would discuss with him whatever caused this rejection. They should have it out, level with Charlie about whatever is bugging them. It's unfair of them to attack Charlie in what they know is his vulnerable point. This attack shows their lack of respect for his feelings.

If you unintentionally hit someone's emotional soft spot, having not been aware of it before, say "I've been insensitive to you and your feelings. This hurt you. Now that you've told me this, I'll attempt being more sensitive to your feelings." When you respect feelings, you keep dialogue flowing. If you don't, dialogue will cease. When someone tells you how they feel, respect their feelings. Avoid making light of them, laughing at them, disregarding them, or, as in the Achilles' heel syndrome, taking advantage of them.

The emotional itch

Have you ever experienced emotional itch? We all undergo this experience because *emotions happen!* We can't avoid experiencing emotions. They happen and just as an itch they can irritate and cause discomfort. When this occurs, we're experiencing emotional itch. What we do about emotions is important. We employ will power in an endeavor to control them, but the emotions are still there. We can dwell on them mentally, causing irritation and building them to greater intensity. Or, we apply the medication of dialogue. In this way we get to the origin, talking them out, venting them, calming the cause of the emotional itch. Once vented, emotions tend to subside. Then we can step back to see problems in proper perspective.

How do we recognize an emotional itch? It takes the form of destructive criticism, secretiveness, excessive talking, withdrawal, gossip, overcautiousness, argumentiveness, or uncooperativeness.

Emotions can be highly volatile. People experiencing intense feelings are often in an irrational mood and aren't receptive to facts. Their emotions must be released and their fears calmed before they can hear facts. An example of this is the subject of the following incident, *Send a Memo?*—

Case Study No. 21 / Send a Memo?

At 11:00 A.M. production manager, Bill Woods, barges by Miss Olive's desk into the office of the president, Jackson Porter.

Miss Olive: But, Mr. Woods, you can't go in there.

Bill: Listen, Miss Olive, you and no one else is gonna keep me out of that office right now. Out of my way!

Jackson: What's all this about, Bill?

Bill: This whole damned campaign is loused up!

Jackson: Really, Bill, I'm busy right now. If you'll send me a memo on whatever it is you're talking about, I'll look it over.

Bill: I don't want to send a memo. I'm burned up!

Jackson: I can't consider any proposals unless they're in writing. You know that. Send a memo, and I'll see what I can do.

Bill: But——

Jackson: Excuse me, I'm busy now.

PROBLEM

Jackson has just capped a volcano that will probably not stay capped. When emotions are running high, it's wise to let the steam blow off and get to the problem.

ALTERNATE APPROACH

Miss Olive: But, Mr. Woods, you can't go in there.

Bill: Listen, Miss Olive, you and no one else is gonna keep me out of that office right now. Out of my way!

Jackson: What's all this about, Bill?

Bill: This whole damned campaign is loused up!

Jackson: Loused up. The campaign?

Bill: The new major product introduction has fallen completely apart. I've just found out that Sales weren't told about the delivery date they could expect the products. I wasn't told when they were starting the major advertising push. Shipping wasn't aware of the urgency. They sent everything by pony express instead of air express.

Then I find the guys in Delivery were asleep. When the boxes came in, they put them back in the warehouses to be unpacked in rotation. Can you believe how all these stupid mistakes can take place?

Jackson: I've got a few ideas, Bill, but I'd like to have your thinking on what went wrong.

Bill: I've got lots to unload! I'd like to unload with some of the other departments involved with this thing.

Jackson: Agreed, Bill. We should have a combined meeting. Can you tell me first what your thinking is right now?

Bill: Well, we've talked before about a critical-path method. We have to have it spelled out in detail, what each person's activities will be, when and where. I think with a time-and-events calendar like this we'll avoid lots of this confusion. I know, I just got a stack of uncoordinated memos from lots of people.

Jackson: What you're saying then is you feel we need a master plan in detail to eliminate inefficiency. You want details spelled out for *everyone* involved.

Bill: You said it! This bit of trying to outguess all the other guys and departments, it doesn't get the job done. We need an interdepartment critical-path method. With that, no one has any excuses for not knowing what he's to do or when he's to do it.

Jackson: I get your message. We can't implement a critical-path method for *this* product introduction, but I'll have Miss Olive contact the group for a meeting here tomorrow morning. We'll see what we can do to salvage and expedite the balance of this campaign. We'll draw up plans *to be specific* in our procedures for future introductions.

Bill: I know there isn't much we can do right now, but if you'll give me some support, I'll try unraveling what we can on the immediate situation this afternoon.

Jackson: Give Miss Olive what you need. We'll do whatever we can.

Bill: Thanks. See you in the morning.

EVALUATION

Jackson has heard Bill out. As a result, something may be done to remedy immediate problems, and prevent a reccurence in the future. Jackson allowed Bill to vent his anger and frustration without trying to stop him.

As we've seen, when emotional interplay flares at a high pitch, little can be accomplished to solve a situation or seek a solution.

When we recognize high emotions, vent them! Get them verbalized. This calms them more quickly and allows fruitful conversation to be resumed. Much of the feeling expressed by us in conversation is a direct result of stimulation by the other party. Unless we respect each other's rights to feelings, an argument is almost inevitable. The other possible result is a total stalemate and/or discontinuation of dialogue. When dialogue intensifies with emotion, a statement such as this may effectively allay an argument: "I respect your right to your opinion and I ask that you respect mine."

Let others know how you feel

We must develop a sensitivity to others, true, but the coin has two sides. The other is, we must allow others to become sensitive to us. When we hide our feelings from people, we aren't giving them an opportunity to know "where we're at." It's necessary to tell a person how you feel. If you don't it's difficult for him to read your mind or feelings. Openness begets openness.

The feelings part of us was there first. When you say, "I feel," it's more encompassing than saying, "I think." Saying, "I think I'm tired," indicates you aren't sure whether or not you're tired. When you say, "I feel tired," I believe you! You can intellectualize about a sentence that's started with, "I think." When you begin a statement with, "I feel," you're on a different level, the understanding level. In this instance you involve your entire self, not just your intellect. Test the difference in meaning of these two sentences. Paul says, "I think I should quit this job." Or, Paul says, "I feel intimidated by the attacks on my integrity." In the first instance he gave what action he wanted to take, what he thought. In the second instance, Paul got to the cause of why he wanted to quit because he expressed his feelings.

When we ask others to reveal their feelings, we have the responsibility to set an example by expressing our feelings, too. Let's look at Paul again. He feels strain between him and a peer. Paul decided to confront him and express how he feels.

He might approach it by saying, "I feel there's a strain in our relationship. I don't know what's caused this strain, but recently we haven't been able to communicate like we used to. What are your feelings about this?"

Paul expresses his feelings and asks for a response on the same level from his peer. What happens after that depends on how honest —open—the parties are in their responses to each other.

Give your feelings to others rather than your judgments. When you give judgments the other person becomes defensive. Keep lines of communication open. Tell him how you *feel* about the statement he made, i.e., "When I hear you talk that way I get a feeling of isolation." This is preferred over the judgmental statement, "No one could like you when you talk that way. You come off sounding like a phony and a louse."

In the first instance you're telling him your reaction to his talk, that he's isolating you with what he's saying. In the second instance, in essence, you're telling him the same thing, only "No one could like you" is judgmental. This tends to turn him off, or cause him to be defensive.

Dr. Lydia Giberson's rules for executive success deal primarily with respecting the person and his feelings.[19] These rules are:

1. Acquire the art of kindliness and persuasion. Kindliness is an attribute of the strong.

2. Put consideration of human dignity above pay, promotion, or environment.

3. Get rid of "double standards of behavior": one for workers, and another for management.

4. Start a request to subordinates with "please." Proper words and actions inspire confidence.

5. Give credit where credit is due. Praise fearlessly. If you must tell somebody off, never do it in front of others. Most people's self-esteem can't take it.

6. Don't be afraid to make changes. If something has been done in a particular way for twenty years, that alone is often a sign that it is being done wrong.

7. In handling grievances, let the employee tell his full story without interruption. A kind word will help.

8. Learn to listen. The occupational disease of a poor executive is inability to listen.

If you keep on the level of feelings, you're more apt to come away with deeper understanding of each other and a renewed strength in friendship. Clear the air (vent feelings and emotions), breathe deeply (discuss the problem), then go on to enjoy a more vigorous relationship. Feelings *do* govern thinking and actions. To create a more comfortable atmosphere and more desirable dialogue, learn to read and respect feelings.

ENJOY SHARING

The need to share

The need to share is instinctive. It's part of human nature, part of being a person identifying with another person. Sharing is belonging. Maslow's hierarchy of human needs[20] indicates the level of belongingness is of major importance to most people after they've satisfied their needs for self-preservation and safety. Then their need is for belongingness, to share.

We identify with people when we feel we can share with them and that they'll share with us. When we share with others and others share with us, we learn. To share says, *"We're a team, we're in there pitching together*, working as a *team* toward accomplishing a *mutual* goal, established for the good of the *group* and the betterment of the *company."* The plural words are the common denominator indicating sharing; to accomplish the plural words in the preceding sentence, it's necessary to share ideas, thoughts, and feelings. It's sharing that creates the cohesive spirit to win, to be better and to produce more, to accomplish quickly and thoroughly the goals and objectives of the group.

When we're active participants in a sport, sharing with the team, we have a better chance to win. We share team signals, we share enthusiasms, we share ideas, we share feelings, we share as a team in victory or defeat. A team doesn't win on the merits of one man alone, it wins on the shared efforts of the team. Even as armchair participants during football season, we share with our favorite team, we become part of every play; we share its injuries, its adulation and/or dejection, its wins and losses. Each member of the team belongs to the team through sharing, and we, in our living room, belong to the team through vicarious sharing.

When we speak of filling the belongingness need, we use plural terms. We replace "I" with "we," "my" with "our," and so on. The plural indicates belonging and sharing of assets as well as liabilities, compliments as well as blame. We work with the plural approach to improve our capacity for sharing, to improve teamwork, and to accomplish "total company" as a concept with our employees.

Honestly shared emotions help to get the work done more easily, better. As a manager, it's wise to begin with yourself. Share your feelings to nurture your employees sharing theirs with you. "This above all, to thine ownself, be true, and it must follow, as the night the day, thou canst not then be false to any man." Shakespeare wrote this and it's still true. Admit your feelings to yourself, then share them with others when you can. It may help to get the job done, because emotions *can* be passed along to co-workers, as the following case indicates. This was cited by Dr. R. B. O'Connor.[21]

. . . I was recently in a session with a section foreman. I had invited him to come down for a medical checkup that was overdue; in the course of it, I asked if he had anything on his mind. The answer came pouring out: Last week, his wife has asked for a divorce. Although he did not get along with her and felt he wouldn't miss her, he was worried sick about the future of their children.

"Doc, how did you guess?" he asked. "Do you have a crystal ball that tells you when people are in trouble?"

Of course, I have no crystal ball. The clue to the problem was simple. Over the past two days, four of this man's subordinates had come separately to the medical department—each one requesting a change of job for medical reasons. One man said he couldn't stand the noise on the job. It was making him tense and nervous, and he couldn't sleep nights. Another said the job was too heavy; at the end of the day his back and legs were aching. Two others said the odors of solvents on the job were nauseating; they couldn't eat their dinner.

These were all long-time employees who had worked in the same section under this supervisor for years. I investigated the physical conditions on the job; nothing had changed. It was at this point that I decided to have a talk with the supervisor.

I didn't give him the names of the men who were requesting transfers, but I did describe their symptoms to him. He began to realize that in his worry over his home situation, he had become so irritable that he was actually making his subordinates sick!

The section was a relatively small one, and it wasn't difficult for the supervisor to get across to his men that he had temporarily been up against a personal problem, but that things would be better in the near future. From that moment on, his section returned to normal. In fact, his men were sympathetic, and they respected his forthrightness. They withdrew their transfer requests, and the productivity of the group returned to the above-normal levels.

A good manager must share experiences with peers, with employer, with employees. Decision making should be a group activity when major policies are involved. Evaluations should be made of individual performance and company procedures. These things are done through sharing. If we aren't apprised of these things, we get the feeling we really don't belong to the total picture, that we're merely an extension of the machine.

We know that feelings influence what a man does and how he does it. It's up to the manager to influence the feelings of his employees. Through sharing in dialogue, he can do this. He influences how an employee feels about himself, his company, his job. As we saw in the preceding case, these things directly influence performance on the job itself. When we encourage others to share their feelings, we'll be better able to grow mutually and to attain mutual goals.

Grapevines and cliques are born out of a need for people to communicate, to belong, to share. Through dialogue they express their feelings, frustrations, ideas, and their concerns. Unless these ingredients of humanity can be shared with a manager, the grapevine can get wormy. Prolonged internal disorder results from a lack of ability to share and express feelings and emotions as they become important.

What are the manager's responsibilities in sharing?

The manager has these factors as his responsibility in sharing.

1. The manager gives reassurance to his employees, peers, and superiors: "I know you can do it!" "You're just the man we need!" "You're improving greatly!" "We can do it, pulling together!" All of us need words of encouragement from time to time. As Bertrand Russell put it, "One can't think hard from a mere sense of duty. I

need little successes from time to time to keep . . . a source of energy."[22] It helps to know someone really has faith in our capabilities. It's good to hear these reassurances verbalized. When a manager shares good words with others, he's a beautiful sensitive human being.

2. The manager nurtures self-respect in his co-workers. People have a high degree of need to be respected by themselves and by others. The manager can help his subordinates to achieve this self-esteem by verbalizing and showing his respect for their feelings and their abilities, their potential. He should strive to recognize the points of interest of others, to recognize their strengths, their achievements. Let them know their importance to the overall projects and products. Look for ways to share good feelings of satisfaction for a job well done. Look for ways to praise people. Through sincere praise we can raise self-esteem. Frequently there's increased productivity on the part of a person who's "high" on self-esteem.

If you're a sales manager, you know that a salesman has a high degree of need for recognition and praise. These are two strong motivators for him. Verbal communication of this is very necessary to him. He'll operate better when he's praised before he goes out to sell *and* when he returns from the sale.

Look for good deeds, make dialogue about them! Let the person know *specifically* why he's so great so he'll continue to grow in this specific area. Instead of saying, "You're doing fine," be specific. "Your draft of the proposal is great!" Specify, specify. The more we offer sincere praise to someone, the more he's able to do for himself—for us!

Simple "Thank you's" are a form of praise—for a job well done, an idea put forth (workable or not), an attempt at a task (completed or not). Recognize effort, endeavor, creativity—this will spawn increased efforts. Recognition is important to self-esteem and highly valued by all human beings, regardless of age or sex. Help yourself by sharing praise with others.

3. The manager encourages cooperation. We must share knowledge and feelings; otherwise no one is sure of his ground, what's expected of him, and what the desires of the other person are. The manager who shares encourages cooperation, and the employee who shares encourages cooperation. The case of *We're Both Wrong* demonstrates this fact:

Case Study No. 22 / We're Both Wrong!

Luke Gordon and Barry Clark are aggressive young salesmen with an automotive wholesale house. The company distributes nationally; both Luke and Barry have central teritories.

For a long time Luke has eyed the company's western territory. He hopes to move there when there's an opening. His wife and children too have indicated a desire to move West. Although Luke is doing well financially where he is, the family would enjoy the warmer climate.

Carl Stevens is national sales manager, having jurisdiction over placement of all key salesmen such as Luke. Carl has just hired a new salesman and is considering putting him into the recently uncovered West Coast area.

Luke and Barry are sitting in the cafeteria of the main factory. and discussing business while enjoying coffee and a Danish.

Barry: You've got a real production quota to make this month, Luke.

Luke: That doesn't bother me. I have good customers. I think they'll respect my suggestions on their orders.

Barry: Did you hear about that new guy getting the West Coast territory?

Luke: You've gotta be kidding!

Barry: No, I just heard about it myself. Pretty nice area.

Luke: You bet it is! That's the prize I was hoping to get.

Barry: I didn't know you wanted it.

Luke: Damned right! So did Connie and the kids. Her family lives out there and we'd hoped to move into that territory when it opened up.

Barry: That's a bastardly shame, Luke.

Luke: Shame! I know what this means. I'm going to quit this stupid company and look for something on the West Coast. I'm sick of this weather here. I know Connie'll go along with my thinking.

PROBLEM

Luke and Carl failed to share thinking and ideas for Luke's future. It's difficult to read minds, so it's important to let one's thinking be known. Share!

There was a breakdown in communications between Luke and Carl. Luke should have shared his objectives with Carl.

ALTERNATE APPROACH

Having just learned that the West Coast territory is open, Luke decided to confront Carl.

Luke: Carl, I'd like to see you a minute. I'm damned upset about some news I just heard.

Carl: Hey, Luke! You look like a storm cloud. What's up?

Luke: My temper's up! I just heard this new guy is being sent to the West Coast territory.

Carl: That's right. The appointment isn't even official yet. You've got a good grapevine to have heard it already.

Luke: I'm really teed off, Carl. The fact is, I've had my eye on that territory ever since I came with the company. My wife and I want to move West.

Carl: I had no idea you wanted to transfer. You've been doing a great job for us here. The customers like you. Your volume is excellent. I thought you were happy with your situation the way it is.

Luke: You *thought!* That's what's wrong, Carl. You did *my* thinking *for me!* Why the hell didn't you *ask me* if I'd be interested in a move?

Harold: You're right, Luke. I made an assumption. I did your thinking for you. I should have gotten the reaction of you and the other senior salesmen. It would have helped me, too, if you'd have indicated your interest in the West.

Luke: Ouch! I deserved that. I should have told you about Connie's parents being out there. I should have told you I'd like to transfer West. I guess I expected you to read my mind, Carl.

Carl: It sounds as though we've both been wrong. Let's see what we can do to change this. As I said, the appointment isn't official yet. I'll ask you now, are you interested in moving to that western territory?

Luke: That sounds like an official invitation, Carl. I accept!

Carl: I think it can be arranged. I don't have the final word, but I'll let you know the outcome by Wednesday.

Luke: I'd like to move with this company, Carl. You've been a good affiliation for me. I'd like to stay with you. I appreciate your doing what you can.

Carl: Call me Wednesday afternoon, and I'll have an answer for you.

EVALUATION

By Luke leveling with Carl, the situation may work out for his transfer. When we encourage cooperativeness, we're saying, "I think well of your abilities and/or position. I appreciate any help you can give me, and I respect your importance as an individual." Had Luke not shared his thinking with Carl, he could have become sullen, uncooperative, and unproductive. As it was, through sharing, his relationship with Carl is more amenable. Chances are, he'll get the territory he wants.

4. The manager averts crisis by sharing. All expressed feelings are *real* to the person expressing them. If they're treated with flippancy or disregard, a barrier is erected in communication. Acknowledge feelings through dialogue. If an employee indicates anger, it isn't stupid to feel angry, or upset, or bored. The manager should acknowledge with, "I hear lots of anger and frustration in what you're saying. Can you share with me what it is that's causing this anger and frustration?" This helps to drain away the poison of intense feelings that can only cloud rationality and intellectual conversation.

When feelings aren't acknowledged, they can cause crisis, they can dissolve to lethargy, eliminate physical and mental energy and strength, and even cloud intelligence. The manager must acknowledge through dialogue to open the channels of communication so essential to physical and mental well-being. This invites a feeling of comfortable ease in our relationship with others. It's also a key to problem solving.

Crisis occurs when an individual is unable to share his feelings and to be "a part of," to belong. *Meanwhile, Two Years Later* expresses the crisis that ensues when sharing doesn't occur:

Case Study No. 23 / Meanwhile, Two Years Later

Peter Barton is a two-year employee of a large corporation. He's a virile, young, energetic, sensitive writer. He reports directly to the head of the public-relations department. Specifically, Peter writes many of the speeches for the president of the company, Mr. Ross.

He's also advance man for him on tours. Peter has just been summoned, for the first time, to Mr. Ross' office.

Mr. Ross: Well, young man, what's this I read in this letter? You've resigned your position with our company?

Peter: That's right, Mr. Ross. I can't take the ivory tower any more. I'm going someplace where people are people.

Mr. Ross: Well, when that's your attitude about us, it's probably better you do leave. Good day!

PROBLEM

Mr. Ross didn't hear any of what Peter was telling him. To begin with, Mr. Ross' insensitivity is evidenced by the fact this is the first time in two years he's met Peter.

ALTERNATE APPROACH

Mr. Ross: Well, young man, what's this I read in this letter? You've resigned your position with our company?

Peter: That's right, Mr. Ross. I can't take the ivory tower any more. I'm going someplace where people are people.

Mr. Ross: You feel you haven't been able to be a person here.

Peter: That's right, Mr. Ross. Do you realize this is the first time in the two years I've been employed here that I've been able to get past the watchdog you have out there? I'm writing *your* speeches, and I've never even met *you* until today! I've been advance man for you, telling people what a remarkable, great genius-guy you are, and all the time knowing I'd never even shaken your hand. I felt like, and I was, a real hypocrite. After the last trip out, I decided I'd had it. That's when I wrote the letter.

Mr. Ross: I hear your frustration, Peter. Sorry about the coldness.

Peter: Coldness? Hell's an iceberg compared to our relationship. I'm really uptight about this, too. I've never known you, yet I've been your voice to thousands of people all over the world. I could have written volumes of better material had I known you. I used to try getting past your sentry out there, but when my boss found out and shot me down for it, I quit trying.

Mr. Ross: It must have been a very frustrating experience for you.

Peter: Precisely! But I'm glad I've finally met you. Before you were only a picture and a title.

Mr. Ross: The past has no excuse. I failed to *let you know* you were doing a good job. I failed to communicate my appreciation. (pause) What's your feeling right now regarding this letter of resignation?

Peter: I don't know. I really don't have a right to feelings at this juncture. I've taken another position. I'll be leaving next week. I wish you'd have let me into your world before. Right now, I'm feeling pretty comfortable with you. The fact remains, I have to move on.

Mr. Ross: I respect your decision, Peter. You're a talented young man. I'll miss having your words to speak. Good luck to you in your future endeavors.

Peter: (Shaking hands warmly) Thank you, Mr. Ross. It's a *pleasure* to have met you. *Sincerely regret* having not had the pleasure before. You're OK.

EVALUATION

Peter communicates his feelings to Mr. Ross. This time, Mr. Ross listens, and is sensitive to them. He allows Peter to express his frustration and to verbalize his complaints.

After the heavy emotions have been exposed, Peter becomes calmly factual and tells Mr. Ross of his disappointment at not knowing him. He makes it clear that had Mr. Ross let him into his world before, he might not be leaving. Yet, there are times when it's too late to salvage a relationship, when there's no alternative but to move on. Crisis happens when we have to say, "If you won't share with me, then I'll have to move on."

5. The manager extends understanding when he shares. He listens to the dialogue of others in an endeavor to understand them, their needs and problems. He doesn't cut them off—or, if he has to cut them off, he still expresses his understanding of their feelings. He should handle the situation in a tactful manner. *The Turn off* gives an example of understanding extended by a manager:

Case Study No. 24 / The Turn off

Neil Richards has been asking for suggestions from his employees so that they may feel more a part of the company, and in turn, the company may profit by these innovations. Max Burns comes rushing into the office of Neil Richards.

Max: Listen, Neil, I've got a great idea! I woke up in the middle of the night. I couldn't go back to sleep. This is a *great* idea. Wait until I tell you about it. It's going to cut production and delivery——

Neil: Listen yourself, Max. I've got a luncheon I have to go to. See me later!

Max: (Thinking to himself as he silently departs Neil's office with his *great* idea disintegrated to atoms) See you later, you bastard! I'll be damned if you think you can turn me on again by just punching a button and *ZAP!* I'll come running back! There are other companies who would jump at this idea. Think I'll call on some of our competition and get their reaction to it. Why not? With you as a boss, who needs poison for the bloodstream? You're a human ulcer-activator! Etc.

PROBLEM

Ideas are valuable to a company. It's impossible to know when one will be just the thing needed in a specific area. Ideas should be listened to.

Neil's icy brusqueness stopped Max's enthusiasm. It killed dialogue immediately. How could Neil handle the situation to preserve Max's dignity, hear out his idea, and still make his luncheon on time? How can Neil dialogue to recognize Max, and turn him down, but not off?

ALTERNATE APPROACH

Max: Listen, Neil, I've got a great idea! I woke up in the middle of the night. I couldn't go back to sleep. This is a *great* idea. Wait until I tell you about it. It's going to cut production and delivery——

Neil: Hold it, Max, just for a couple of hours, can you? I hear lots of enthusiasm about what must be a *great* idea to have you this excited. I want to hear about what might cut production and delivery costs. But, I'm just on my way out to another appointment. Get my secretary to make an appointment for you right after lunch. I'll listen eagerly then. Hang on to that idea, will you? I'll see you in a couple of hours. Thanks.

Max: (Thinking to himself as Neil hurries by him, and he heads toward the secretary) OK. I'll make the appointment for after lunch, I guess I can hang on to my ideas until then. It won't be easy, but wait until I tell Neil my plan. I know it'll work. I don't understand why we didn't see it before. When we . . . .

EVALUATION

In less time than a sixty-second commercial, Neil had dignified his employee. It takes only moments to extend an understanding word to someone. To share his feelings, even briefly, lets him know that you're aware of his existence. Expressing understanding is of major significance to the overall good relationships that are to be enjoyed in the business world.

6. The manager accepts, as part of the process of sharing. "To err is human, to forgive is divine." When an individual shares with his manager and expresses weakness, or wrong deeds, or guilt, it's up to the manager to accept these things and treat them with forgiveness. When people confide and their trust is belied, or they're threatened with the information they've divulged, they aren't apt to confide in the future. A manager must learn to accept what's shared with him. When necessary, forgive and forget.

7. The manager shares joy! Blake wrote, "Exuberance is beauty!" It can make a day! Share joy in the day's activities, share news of a bonus or a promotion, whatever it might be. Joy and happiness are contagious. Share good feelings and help others to feel good. Share your success, praise success in others. It gives all pleasure and lightens the burdens of the day.

What's so eternally serious about the business world that people feel they have to submerge their sense of humor or they'll be thought insincere and flippant? A good laugh is great exercise and a seldom-thing in our uptight society. In dialogue, let humor have its place, and everyone will feel better exercised. A good laugh often clears tensions and electricity from the air; then participants can back off from the problem and attack it with renewed spirit and a fresh outlook. Often when things are tense, the ability to share laughter is just the thunderbolt needed to clear the air. Laughing at oneself, at one's shortcomings, or at incidents that have been humorous *can* save the day! Good dialogue allows much latitude for levity. Let laughter release tensions.

A verse on a greeting card reads, "Cheer up, the sun is just behind a cloud." That's the way it is in nature and that's the way it is in life. Dialogue can be the wind that dispels the clouds of confusion and frustration in everyday life to let the sun shine through. An interview can begin with the interviewee uptight, but with effective dialogue and a shot of good humor, it can end with a warm handshake and a smile. Every problem has within it the seed of solution. Dialogue and a sense of humor can locate that seed so that participants can proceed with a positive course of action. Share the joy, humor, and sunshine—let others enjoy joy.

Don't be afraid to express happy feelings; it isn't childish—it's adult! It shows the capacity to be human, to display happiness. But it must be sincere.

What the manager reaps in return for sharing

Sharing creates a two-way relationship. Hopefully the outgrowth will be respect, trust, and understanding. Without sharing, we're apt to deteriorate a relationship to distrust, rejection, needling, sarcasm, depression, ridicule. Sharing ideas and respecting feelings are ways of gaining confidence with a superior, peers, or with an employee. To continue dialogue, you must gain the confidence of people. Your communication falls on deaf ears if the receiver doesn't first give you his confidence. When you share, you confide in someone, you're telling him you trust him. When you ask him to share his opinion, you're subtly complimenting him, his integrity and judgment—you're telling him you trust him. When there's no trust, people don't want to share information and opinions—there's a feeling of fear.

The most effective way for us to gain insight into our *self* is to cultivate relationships of respect and trust, to invite candor and give candor in return. This is true sharing, true respect, true friendship.

PHASE III

Forces
of
Dialogue

THE ART OF QUESTIONING

Some manager-uses for questions

The dialogist manager starts his discussions by asking questions. Contrary to the monologist authoritarian manager who *tells* his listeners what *he* wants them to hear, the dialogist manager involves his people through asking questions. He'll *ask* for help. He *asks* for thinking. He *asks* for cooperation. "Asking of" evokes positive responses more quickly than "demanding from." People don't resent being *asked* as readily as they resent being *told*. Being told is an indication of a parent-child relationship. Asking is an indication of an adult-adult relationship.

Adult-adult: "Will you make these corrections in your report, please?"

Parent-child: "Do these corrections. This report is sloppy this way!"

Chances are the asking technique of adult-adult will get the job done faster and with better feelings than the parent-child one wherein the person is told to do a job.

1. *Asking with questions:* Since people resent being *told*, how can we activate them to participate in dialogue? By letting them come up with their own ideas. We tend to like our own ideas best. The temptation is to set our own thinking forth as the way things should be done. However, by employing questions and asking for another's thinking and ideas, there may be a better way suggested by someone else.

Instead of telling your department personnel that they have to cut their budget, why not call them together and pose as a problem that there's a critical need to cut the budget? Ask them to draw up a plan as to how they can participate in accomplishing the reduction of costs. This poses it as a question to them—a challenge for them to work out. This enlists their cooperation to solve a problem.

2. *Discovering the catalyst:* How can you locate the catalyst in a group of workers? Observe the group when they're together. Watch for the one who is a question asker. Usually this is your catalyst.

He asks good questions, sound, meaningful questions: "How can we improve production and cut time?" "Would we make a better product if we used copper here?" He asks creative questions that are action oriented and directed toward improvement. Listen for this person. He's a valuable asset (or a bitter enemy). Listen for him, listen to him, encourage him, *profit through him!*

3. *Criticizing through questions:* We've talked of dialogue as a means of criticism. A point here regarding this: When you *tell* someone what a bad job he's doing, your reprimand deflates the fellow's self-esteem. Instead, could you ask him how he thinks he can do a better job? This leaves his self-esteem intact. It gives him room to exploit his own difficulties.

Adult-adult "How do you think you can improve your production?"

Parent-child: "Your production is lousy. You've got to raise it!"

Through the adult-adult tactic, you allow his replies to establish (a) what his problem is, (b) what he can do about it, and (c) how he will implement this knowledge into action. This is criticizing through questions.

4. *Stimulating creativity and innovation:* Questions can and do stimulate creativity and innovation. Creativity is triggered by curiosity. As children we improvised many things through our imagination. As adults we can improvise and devise new and better ways "how to," but usually only when we're prodded to do so. The difference between childhood and now is, as adults we have better know-how then we had as children, but we've stifled it under the camouflage of adult "sophistication." To unlock this natural talent, it becomes the responsibility of a manager to ask "How can we . . . ?" "When can we . . . ?" "What do you think . . . ?" etc. The energizer for creativity is the same at any age; it is curiosity, the curiosity to explore, invent, take apart, and put back together. A manager can stimulate this creativity by asking for people's thinking, then he sets into motion the same challenges that we had as children. Our curiosity is piqued to explore, invent, take apart, and to put back together again.

5. *Re-directing thinking:* When attempting to get someone to abandon or re-direct his way of thinking and accept another course or alternative, first ask him to define and outline his position. You'll poison the conversation if you reply, "You're wrong!" or if you

ignore his point of view and go on with, "This is the way I see it!" After he has fully expressed his thinking, he can become receptive to what you may have to say, to your point of view. Then you're ready to state your ideas and thinking. After you have established your premise, again ask questions to affirm the other person has received your ideas correctly. As Dr. Jesse S. Nirenberg states in his book, *Getting Through to People*:[23]

> Since a question is a request for information, in order to supply it the other person has to move from the passive, listening state to the active, thinking one. He has to reach in his mind for the answer or perhaps work it out. Then he has to put it into language in order to communicate it. If the question you ask him is related to something you just told him, you are making his mind work on your ideas.
>
> Keep in mind that the telling of something is only the first step in getting it across. In order to absorb your ideas the listener has to mentally react to them; and you have to ask him to react.

As a manager, there are many times when questions will give you the answers to your problems. They'll help you in expressing your interest in others. They say that you care enough about others to ask about them and their problems, their needs, and their thinking. Questions help you to raise a man's self-esteem. In his eyes, you're indicating respect for his thinking. You're saying that you hold him in esteem. Through questions you tell others you trust and respect them, that you'd like them to share their intelligence with you.

Fundamentals of dialogical questioning

There's an art to asking questions. You can ask random questions and get random answers. To obtain the response you're looking for, and to become skillful in this art, there are certain techniques involved.

To prepare your dialogue, it's helpful to categorize questions. There are many ways of doing this, but for convenience let's give them four labels:

1. SIMPLE: *Simple questions are those that require a short, concise reply.* Generally they evoke a one- or two-word response. They seldom require thinking on the part of the receiver. Usually, the answers to these questions will be familiar and easy for the receiver to deliver. Simple questions would include: "Hello?" "What

time is it?" "What's your name?" "Do you think it will rain?" "Hot today, isn't it?" These are simple questions requiring a simple, short answer.

They can be overused. If strung together in a long series, they can drive a person up a tree, or out of the room. It's easy to become *uneasy* with too many of these questions fired at you in repetition. You may have a feeling you're on the witness stand. The following is an example of a too-long series of simple questions.

Sam: Hi, Ron.

Ron: Hi.

Sam: Nice day, isn't it?

Ron: Yep.

Sam: Have any luck yesterday?

Ron: No.

Sam: Any appointments for today?

Ron: One.

Sam: Where?

Ron: Here.

Sam: Think he'll buy your idea?

Ron: Doubtful.

Sam: How's your wife?

Ron: Fine.

Sam: And the kids?

Ron: OK.

Sam: Well, I guess I'd better be going.

Ron: Bye.

Sam: Bye.

The questions asked got monosyllablic answers because they didn't ask for thinking on Ron's part. He just replied very simply and easily. This type of question has its place, but it must be combined with other types of questions to be effective and interesting.

2. STIMULATING: *Stimulating questions ask for thoughts and ideas and feelings.* They're difficult, if not impossible to answer with a simple yes or no. As an example:

"What's your thinking about this type of policy?" (Asks for the thinking of a person.)

"What's your feeling about that proposal?" (Asks for the feelings.)

"What's your idea for a production forecast for next year?" (Asks for ideas.)

Stimulating questions and Simple questions are good ways to introduce conversation. They stimulate the other person's thinking and encourage his participation in the exchange of ideas. But to avoid the long string of simple questions, let's compare the two and see how the same sentence can be changed from a simple (a yes or no reply) to a stimulating (some thought goes into the reply).

Simple	*Stimulating*
"Do you like your boss?"	"How do you feel about working for your present boss?"
"Would your manager approve?"	"How do you think your manager would react to the proposal?"
"Do you approve?"	"How do you react to that statement?"
"What's wrong?"	"Could you tell me something more about why you disagree?"
"Do you have any friends?"	"Will you tell me about some of your friends?"
"You're depressed?"	"What do you mean when you say depressed?"
"You don't agree?"	"Can you spell out your objections?"
"You're mad?"	"Can you describe the incident that caused your anger?"

With the stimulating question you get the attention of your listener and activate his thinking. You challenge him to become more involved since you're requesting a reply. The stimulating question is a real thought prodder.

Talk shows on television have gained great popularity. Their acceptance (and ratings) seem to be commensurate with the type of questions that the host asks of his guests. Most of the questions are designed to evoke a story rather than just a few words in reply. These are some of the questions David Frost asked of Robert Mitchum in a ninety-minute TV interview:

"What's the very first thing you remember when your family moved south?"

"What actually did you have to do at that time?"

"Were there any other characters like that in those days?"

"What did you learn from him?"

"What kind of guys were riding the freight trains in those days?"
"What do you remember of the experience?"
"At that time what did you think you'd be doing?"
"How would you describe the character you play?"
Each question asked by David Frost was a stimulating question. With this type of question, you're reaching for information through mental contact.

3. SAME: *Same questions are effective as a means of requesting amplification and clarification of a point.* Same questions repeat two or three words from the last sentence just spoken by the other person. You repeat the *same* words that have been said in question form. This, too, can be overdone when they're the only type of question used. Two in succession is the most that should be used at one time. *Good conversation is an exchange of ideas.* Using the same type of question repetitiously shuts off exchange.

Look at the incorrect way, with several same questions in series:
Nick: What sort of position do you hold in your company, Ray?
Ray: I'm in production.
Nick: Production?
Ray: Yes, I work with developing ideas.
Nick: Developing ideas?
Ray: Yes, we take the suggestions of customers and research and consider them.
Nick: Suggestions?
Ray: Yes, through consumer research, we get feedback.
Nick: Feedback?
Ray: Feedback is the result of test markets and research.
Nick: Test markets?
Ray: Yes, you nut! How come all of these questions? What are you, some kind of spy?

It's easy to see that a continuous string of these same questions can be irritating. Let's see how it can be effective in producing an exchange of ideas with same questions in combination with other types.
Nick: What sort of position do you hold in your company, Ray?
Ray: I'm in production.
Nick: Production?
Ray: Yes, I work with developing ideas to be incorporated into new products.
Nick: Great! Research and production? Without you fellows, there

might not be much product improvement. Where do you get most of your new ideas, Nick?

Ray: From several sources. Basically they come from our research scientists and from the public itself.

Nick: From the public? Do you mean I help you design your new products?

Ray: In a sense you do. And so do many other consumers. We run test markets on things. Market research does a survey of the area and reports the findings back to us.

Same questions can stimulate conversation, clarify misunderstood points, and ask for elaboration on a point for development and amplification.

4. SUBSTITUTE: *Substitute questions help in obtaining clarification and verification of another's words.* The fourth classification of questions is the one least used in our society. With a substitute question we re-state what's been said by someone, substituting our words for theirs. We're asking for affirmation that we've interpreted their statement correctly.

Terry: It's my feeling Vance shouldn't be included.

Sims: Let me be sure I understood what you just said. You're saying you veto Vance becoming an active participant at our management meetings?

Terry: Well, not exactly. I just don't think he should be at all of our management meetings, not right now.

Sims: Can you make a more definite statement, Terry? "All" and "right now"? Could you define those terms?

There'll be times when using the substitute question we'll discover what *was said* and what *we interpret it to mean* are two different things. By re-stating *in our own words*, both parties may realize neither understands the other and there's a need for clarification. Or, we may find we both mean substantially the same thing. At that point the conversation can proceed.

When several people are engaged in dialogue, this device can be particularly meaningful. It's difficult to keep understanding clear between two people. When more are involved, it's more difficult. The more minds attempting to comprehend an idea, the more possibility for misinterpretation of meanings. Therefore, it's essential to clarify certain statements with substitute questions, asking for affirmation or for amplification.

The following case gives examples of all four types of questions:

Case Study No. 25 / That's Just Part of It.

Doug Finley works in a publishing house. He's been very upset recently, or so it would seem. He's sulked and said nothing to anyone. Finally, Carey Brant, his editor, decides he can't take the silent treatment any longer and confronts him at his desk.

Carey: Is something wrong with you, Doug?
Doug: No.
Carey: Are you feeling all right?
Doug: Sure.
Carey: Is there something wrong with your job?
Doug: No.
Carey: Can I do anything to help you?
Doug: No.
Carey: Is there anything you'd like to talk about?
Doug: No.
Carey: Well, if there is, let me know.
Doug: OK.

PROBLEM

The type of questions that Carey asked were hardly thought provoking for Doug. He was able to remain aloof from involvement or commitment because the questions required only a simple "yes" or "no" monosyllable-type response.

ALTERNATE APPROACH

Carey: How are things going with you, Doug? (Simple)
Doug: OK.
Carey: What project are you working on now? (Stimulating)
Doug: I'm proofing the manuscript for that new cookbook.
Carey: How much longer do you think you'll be on that? (Stimulating)
Doug: I'll probably be finished with it this week.
Carey: How do you feel about proofing? (Stimulating)
Doug: It isn't very creative.
Carey: What would you enjoy doing other than proofing, Doug? (Stimulating)
Doug: Well, I guess it would be more stimulating if I could be in on the selection of manuscripts.

Carey: Is what you're telling me, that you feel bored with just proofing all the time? (Substitute)

Doug: I guess that's what I mean. I really hadn't thought of it that way. But that's just part of it.

Carey: "Part?" (Same)

Doug: Well, I'd like to do some writing, too. If I could work with some author revising and rewriting, that would be great. The idea of being in on evaluating the manuscripts when they come in, I'd find that challenging. Or, writing the jackets. When I came here I had no idea I'd be stuck proofing forever! I thought my job would entail these other things, too. Every time a promotion comes along, I realize, I won't get it because I've never had the chance to show what I can do. I'd like to be somebody, not just a proofreader like I am now. All I'm asking for is the chance. If I don't make it, then I'll accept that.

Carey: Doug, I've learned more about you in these few minutes than in all the time you've worked here. Thanks for opening up with me. Let's see what we can do to get you out of this lethargy and get you involved with some more creative challenge.

Let me talk it over with our office manager. Stop to see me on Friday, say about two. We'll re-evaluate your job, what you're going to do, and where you can expect to go.

Doug: Thanks, Carey—thanks! I've got to say something to you. I never thought you cared about your employees. But, I'm changing my mind.

Carey: See you at two on Friday!

EVALUATION

When opening his discussion, Carey asked easy-to-answer questions about things that were familiar to Doug. After getting some responses from him, Carey proceeded to ask questions that would evoke feelings and thinking from him to get him to level. Through proper questioning, Carey can now help Doug with his problems.

Questions can open the floodgate to a person's mind.

Purpose and function of questions

Having four classifications of questions as a base from which to work, what questions do we ask where? First, we must establish our purpose. What aim do we want to accomplish with our dialogue? What's the goal we're striving to achieve through our questions? It might be to discover why the decreased production on our line? It might be an endeavor to understand the needs of an individual in our employ. Possibly we want to get a decision from another department about their participation in a new campaign. In dialogue, we must have a goal, a purpose, to which we direct our questions and responses. Now we're ready to design our manner of approach through questions. To do this, we need to become familiar with the function questions perform for us.

The function of questions is to:

1. *Establish rapport:* This is the "Hello" of our encounter. It's comparable to the introduction of a speech. Think back to the fraternity social. You were establishing rapport with simple, easy questions. They served the purpose of setting the climate and just getting comfortable with someone else. The type of question most used here is simple. We're looking for short, concise answers for the most part. We attempt putting others at ease by asking questions to which they can respond easily.

Suppose we've met this person before? We aren't literally saying hello for the first time. It's common practice, even with people who know each other very well, to open conversation with warm-up words. These define the mood of the other person—what their "temperature" is at the time of our meeting. First time or seventieth, there's usually some short greeting to effect establishing rapport at the immediate time and place.

2. *Probe for needs and problems:* "Now that I've said hello, I want to know more about you." The aim of these questions is to understand more about a person and/or a situation. We'll use stimulating and same questions here for the most part. We're looking for needs and problems that will become the focal point for the balance of the discussion. Most of this area is governed by questions that say: "What's your problem?" "What can I do to help you with your problem?" "Where can we coordinate our efforts to meet your needs?" "How can I contribute to your project?" Through questions such as these we discern the needs and problems of others. We note what part we may play in their solution. Until we know another's needs, it's difficult to know what direction to take. If we've perceived these needs in advance of our meeting, we might state

them, asking for affirmation through our questions: "If I understand correctly, the purpose of our meeting is to discuss the forthcoming budget forecast?" In this area we're focusing on the needs (problem) of the individual. This keeps irrelevant, extraneous material from consuming valuable business time.

3. *Share thinking and ideas:* "What do you really think?" "What are your ideas about this problem?" "How do you feel about it?" Here we attempt to understand the inner person. Again we'll use same and stimulating questions, since we're looking for opinions and for clarification. Our questions might take this form: "What's your thinking about the recent breakthrough in the analgesic field?" "What do you think we can do to establish a better climate for our managers?" "Training sessions?" "Job enrichment?" "How do you feel about next week's board meeting?"

We'll find this area rich for stimulating creativity. "What's your opinion?" "How can we do this more efficiently?" Through questions we unlock creative thinking. It's better to have fifty times thinking power than one thinking power. The manager of 50 people can have this fifty times strength in creativity if he'll ask meaningful questions of his subordinates.

4. *Uncover objections:* "Do you agree, or disagree?" "If you disagree, why?" "What are your objections?" We're attempting to see where both sides stand. We've said hello, established certain needs and problems, expressed ideas and thinking. Now it's time to find out where both of us stand on the issues presented. Here we'll use all four types of questions. We want to be specific and precise in detail (simple); we want to obtain additional ideas (stimulating); we want to amplify things that have been said (same); we must be sure we both mean the same thing by what we're saying (substitute).

SIMPLE: "The price should be quoted at $10.70 per unit?"

STIMULATING: "What additional suggestions can you offer for ways to improve this product?"

SAME: "Industrial advertising?"

SUBSTITUTE: "What you're saying is, you feel there hasn't been sufficient research to warrant marketing the new product in February?"

These questions at this point may define the specifics of time, place, amount, and so forth. They'll serve to *get further thinking* that might not have been verbalized before. These questions should *clarify* what's meant by both parties so there's no misunderstanding due to misinterpretation of words.

5. SUMMARY: "What have we said?" "What points do we agree and/or disagree on?" "How should we proceed?" "What's our path of action?" We want to recap the points that have been made; state what our resolutions are; and establish how we're going to implement them. We'll ask such things as: "If I understand you correctly, you're suggesting a re-alignment of salaries for all middle and top management?" Or, "You're proposing then, that we attempt to open our European market by November of this year?" Or, "Let me feedback the dates that involve my department. Are these correct?" "When do I announce the travel plans for the award winners?" This is the wrap-up of the conversation. It should allow both (all) parties to have clear understanding of what problems are involved, what measures have been suggested as solutions, and what the plans are for action.

Dr. Jesse Nirenberg suggests: "Skillfully put questions can guide another person's thinking far more persuasively than the most logical argument. Moving another person's thinking by questioning is probably as old as human discourse."[24]

The following case points up the factors that have been presented regarding both the types of questions and their functions:

Case Study No. 26 / Christmas Bonus?

Ed Parker is office manager for a large advertising firm. He's just been called into the office of his boss, Chet Randolph, for a discussion.

Chet: Sit down, Ed. There's a little matter I'd like to discuss with you.

Ed: That's what your note said. What's happening?

Chet: The order has come down to cut costs on overtime in your department. For all the overtime being put in, seemingly, no more work is being turned out. You'll have to control this somehow. Cut it out, but get the work done. I don't care what you do, but my head is on the block and I don't intend losing it!

Ed: I don't know what I can do about it, but I'll see.

Chet: Get back to me as soon as you can!

PROBLEM

Chet was direct in his approach, getting right to the problem—costs and his neck. He was *too* direct in this instance. The way he presented the problem had the sound of a threat. He didn't give Ed a chance to suggest what he felt was the cause of the problem or how he would propose solving it. Most of what Ed heard was Chet's threat that he was to save *Chet's* neck!

ALTERNATE APPROACH

Chet: Sit down, Ed?

Ed: Thanks.

Chet: How are things going in your department?

Ed: OK, I guess. No complaints on my part, anyway.

Chet: On *your* part? Are there complaints among your personnel?

Ed: Oh, nothing other than the usual, I suppose.

Chet: The usual?

Ed: I get resistance from the crew on some things. They don't seem to cooperate fully on some projects the way I think they should.

Chet: Can you be more specific?

Ed: Well, there's one individual, the ringleader in the group. We're always at odds about something, it seems. I have a feeling it's a personality clash, as the old copout goes.

Chet: Have you talked to him about this?

Ed: Yes, but I get nowhere. The whole problem revolves around the fact that as the catalyst goes so go the followers. It's gotten to the point I think they're stalling about getting material out.

Chet: Could this be the reason for so much overtime being charged to your department?

Ed: It could very well be. It seems there are always ways for them to sabotage getting things out during regular business hours. That means overtime to meet deadlines.

Chet: Have you heard anything else that might indicate there's something we don't know about?

Ed: Nothing of any current happenings. The last major incident was over the Christmas bonus. But that's been months ago. Since the holiday, nothing's been said about it. Other than clashes with the ringleader, things have been routine.

Chet: Hmmmm. That's interesting. Look at this payroll report for your group. I have a record here for the last year. When did the incident occur about the Christmas bonus?

Ed: It was just about Thanksgiving time when it started.

Chet: And it was just before Christmas they found out they weren't getting one, right?

Ed: Yes.

Chet: Take a look at this graph line.

Ed: Will you look at that chart! There it is. The overtime went up right after that! Slowly at first, and it's been increasing ever since. I don't believe my eyes. I've heard of this sort of thing, but I haven't had it happen to me, ever!

Chet: What you're saying is, they decided to drag their work out during the day, make it stretch into overtime, and by doing that, they'll earn what they'd have gotten in bonus?

Ed: It looks like that's the story.

Chet: There's the answer to the overtime problem, Ed. Those characters are going to get their Christmas extra even if it means overtime.

Ed: Then it really hasn't been a personality clash *per se*. This seems to be a conspiracy. That's what's at the base of the whole problem—it's the *real* problem. Obviously, attitudes are commensurate with the end-goal, and their goal is to be uncooperative!

Chet: Ed, old buddy, you've got a problem!

Ed: You're telling me! Now I've got to unravel it. I want you to know right now, any suggestions you have—don't keep them to yourself.

Chet: Let's both give this some thought. I'm free tomorrow morning at ten. Can we meet then?

Ed: You bet. Meanwhile, I think I'll make another appointment —with the leaders of the group. I want to put this thing on the table and get it cleared up.

Chet: The sooner the better. See you at ten?

Ed: Right!

EVALUATION

What appeared to be the trouble was only a symptom of the real cause. Chet's deeper probing with stimulating questions uncovered the clash between the catalyst and Ed. Another level of probing revealed the Christmas bonus to be the real problem. Two heads *are* better than one. When Chet and Ed put their heads together, they found the original cause for the overtime in Ed's department.

The leader using questions

When functioning as group leader, a good warm-up technique is to ask questions. This involves the group, stimulating their thinking. It makes them participants rather than spectators. *Warning: A mistake that the leader often makes is to begin his session with: "Are there any questions among the group?" Or, "Is there anything you'd like to discuss?" These are simple questions and it's easy for the group to respond with silence or a simple negative "no." It's much more effective when the leader uses stimulating questions. He asks for thinking on the part of the group, with participation in response.* The stimulating question can open floodgates for the leader: "What's your thinking regarding the proposal to air-condition the cafeteria?" "How do you feel about the commission plan for employees?" This type of question will activate thinking and it's more apt to evoke response.

The same principle holds true regarding the close of a meeting when a leader says: "Any questions?" If the response is silence, he'll conclude the session with "Well, if there are no questions we'll adjourn." It might be more meaningful if he were to ask stimulating questions regarding some of the points either he or the group has presented. This will serve two purposes: It will act as a recap of the session, and it will tell the leader whether or not the major issues of the meeting were understood by the group.

When a monologue becomes a dialogue

There's a place for lecture material in business. This may be a formal lecture (speaker and audience), or it might take the form of a lengthy speech (presentation) at a group meeting. Whichever, this type of speech tends to become a real monologue: "I'm here to tell you—and this is the way it is!"

The presentation will not become lethal-lulling if questions and participative answers are used frequently within its context. People can stay with a lengthy dissertation better, following it with more interest, when questions are interspersed to challenge and direct their thinking. The following material is an example of a speech containing questions designed to keep the listeners' thinking involved with the flow of words:

Is the *manner* in which a question is delivered of importance? Indeed, the manner is of prime importance. It should be considered equally as important as the content of the questions. Why? Because a question delivered in an angry tone evokes a different response from the same question delivered in a jovial tone. What about expressions of the face? They're vital to acceptance of the question, too. A smile on your face brings a more pleasant meaning to your verbal delivery. Say the same question with a scowl and you'll literally say something different—the same words but the meaning is different because of the countenance. What about the rest of the body? The total appearance affects what is said. A question asked while fidgeting with a pen or looking out the window may indicate boredom or a lack of sincerity. Composure and looking someone in the eye gives a totally different meaning to your questions. It connotes honesty, sincerity, and concern. So, is the whole person important to what's being said? You bet! From eye contact to tone of voice to choice of words, to inflection —all are a part of the questions you ask. ALL are important.

Five questions were interspersed in the preceding paragraph. They were used to introduce new topics, to ask for clarification, to summarize. It takes concentrated, conscious awareness to become adept at this type of communication, to have it smooth-flowing in presentation. If it's stilted it will be ineffective. How can you become proficient with it? Like most things, repetitive practice, practice, practice.

THE CYBERNETICS OF DIALOGUE

Without total listening there can be no fruitful conversation. It precedes knowledge and predisposes us to understanding. It equips us with factual information and involves us with underlying emotional meanings. It gives us an insight into others and to ourselves. It involves us with another human being, to relate, through listening, to another's thoughts, ideas, and emotions. Through successful listening we stabilize interpersonal communications.

Emerson wrote: "Every man I meet is my master in at least one thing and in that I hope to learn from him." Through listening to others, we can learn. As listeners we become professional eavesdroppers on the ideas, attitudes, and emotions of other human beings. J. C. Penney was reputedly always a good listener. He felt that many men fail to achieve success because they've never learned to listen.

Listening is the cybernetics of dialogue, it's the corrective mechanism of conversation. It obtains data, then acts on it to keep the speaking on a clear channel. It's the guidance system of dialogue. We take into our listening computer, for the most part, that which interests us and stimulates our emotions and affects our feelings; therefore, we can say that listening is greatly subjective. We tend to hear that which we can identify and that to which we can relate. We set our "computer" to reject information that doesn't please us. Listening, because of its subjective nature, can come to an impasse unless we listen with mutuality and understanding to what's being said. We need to set our computer to listen with flexibility; otherwise we're apt to reach a stalemate, an impasse in our conversation.

How total listening benefits managers

When managers become astute listeners, they can become more effective with their subordinates, with their peers, and with their superiors. The manager is the belt line of the hourglass of business. Through him filters information regarding company policy, production, and so forth—from his superiors downward to the subordinates; from the subordinates upward to management. The manager is the filter to transmit relevant, important information upward or downward and to stop that which is irrelevant. As the belt line of an organization he must listen totally to convey correct information.

The concerned manager, through his attentive listening, (1) gives support to people to orient their thinking toward company objectives; (2) helps his subordinates to crystallize their thinking; (3) guides personnel to think through their needs; and (4) becomes a sounding board helping others to verbalize their thoughts. He must listen for cues that hide beneath the surface of words. He becomes accomplished at finding subsurface evidence that will indicate to him the real needs. He listens for motives, feelings, and attitudes that are concealed beneath the facade of business protocol and etiquette.

The effective manager discovers seemingly extraneous comments and remarks that are often arrows pointing to the real problems. These remarks are usually out of the order of logical thinking. It's then his duty to draw the other person out, to discern why the extraneous matter was introduced into the conversation and what relevance it has to the major subject.

The following case points up getting beneath the surface through effective listening.

Case Study No. 27 / Let Me Out!

Leo Stewart has been a dynamo of a salesman for seventeen years. He came up the ranks in his company, becoming a leader in the national sales force. His income and position were substantial. To effect his advancement he was brought into the home office as vice-president in charge of sales, a better salary and title. Leo has spent eight months in this capacity.

Today he telephones his immediate superior, Eric Ashton, and asks to lunch with him.

Leo: Thanks, Eric, for managing to have lunch with me today.

Eric: No problem. Or, now that I've said that, *is* there a problem, Leo? You're playing with that spoon like you're trying to re-shape it.

Leo: Not really. I'm just a little tense.

Eric: Things are going OK for you, aren't they?

Leo: Sure, sure. Well, you see, the truth of the matter is, I haven't been feeling very well lately.

Eric: Oh? That's too bad. Careful what you order. You'd better see about a company physical. You're a valuable man. Can't afford to have you sick!

Leo: You're right. I'll make an appointment for a physical right after lunch. Let's order. I'll be OK. Just nerves.

PROBLEM

Eric hasn't listened to the "nerves" Leo is displaying. Something is causing his tensions, yet Eric is parentally intellectualizing that Leo should have a physical. He should be listening for the underlying meaning of Leo's nerves.

ALTERNATE APPROACH

Leo: Thanks, Eric, for managing to have lunch with me today.

Eric: No problem. Or, now that I've said that, *is* there a problem, Leo? You're playing with that spoon like you're trying to re-shape it.

Leo: Not really. I'm just a little tense.

Eric: Things are going OK for you, aren't they?

Leo: Sure, sure. Well, you see, the truth of the matter is, I haven't been feeling very well lately.

Eric: Not feeling well?

Leo: No. I guess it's just nerves.

Eric: What's causing the nerves? Is there anything you'd like to discuss? Any particular problem you'd like to share?

Leo: Well, that's really why I wanted to lunch with you, Eric. You know I've been here in this office for eight months now. All during this time I've felt like a salesman out of business. I'm in a cage. I just feel like I'm not at home here and I don't know what the hell I'm doing most of the time.

Eric: Do you feel you want more support from me? Or an assist from someone who's more familiar with procedures here?

Leo: No. At first, I thought that was the problem. But everyone has been very helpful, especially you! It just seems I can't adjust to the confinement.

Eric: What would you like to do about this situation, Leo?

Leo: I'd like to tell all of the protocol, and the waste of time, and nit-picking and humdrum reports, and memos, to go to hell! Just let me get back to my people in the field!

Eric: Those are pretty strong feelings you're expressing. It sounds as though it's more than the confinement that's bothering you.

Leo: Of course, it is. It's the whole bunch of hingeheads, and the "After you, Alphonse!" and "No, after you!" That's the stuff that's driving me up the wall! Plus the tremendous amount of wasted time I see going on because someone has to wait to have a stupid memo signed before he can go to the john. It takes forever to see results of any project or plan here. I like it out there where the action is.

Look, when I make a sale I know it's made *then*, or shortly afterward. I see the smile on a customer's face when I service his account properly. I know my clients, and they know me.

Here, I don't think anyone knows anyone. Everyone's afraid to death of his job, and that's why they don't open their mouths to be real people.

Eric: I hear every word you're saying, Leo. And I respect your right to your feelings. Is there some place I—we have let you down? The company home office really isn't that dastardly—that's *my* opinion. I've been used to it, though, for a long time.

Leo: Maybe you're right, but I'm uncomfortable here. I don't want to stay in this position any longer. I've tried to make it work. Maybe I haven't tried long enough. But I'm convinced that's what's causing the nerves and tension.

Eric: What would you like to do about this, Leo?

Leo: If you'll agree, Eric, I'd like to be transferred back to the field. My decision to come here was one of good intent, but it was just one of those bad decisions.

Eric: If that's your conclusion, then I'll abide by it. I respect your thinking and I'm sure you've considered what the move entails, including salary and title. We'll lose a good man from here, but at least the company isn't losing a top salesman.

If you'll put this in writing for me after lunch, then we'll talk about where you'd like to transfer and we'll process the arrangements.

Leo: Thank you, Eric. Sorry I blew my stack to you. I appreciate your understanding.

EVALUATION

The *real* problem was discovered and resolved. It's imperative that a manager listen intensely to whatever is said to him. Any problem that's presented to him *is a problem!* It may appear minimal to the manager, but to the person experiencing it, the problem may seem like it's Goliath and he's David. Listen with a sympathetic attitude, being careful not to dismiss the matter with a "Forget it," "That's nothing," "Don't be silly," or "Don't worry about it." Help the person to talk it out and to seek his own solution.

OBSERVATION

This case exemplifies the "square peg in the round hole." If someone is adamant about his feelings, frequently it's better for him to change jobs rather than accept further discomfort staying where he isn't satisfied. Some men are born to sell, others to manage! What's wrong with letting them do just that?

A manager should listen to the true concerns of subordinates and peers. In this way he learns the needs of his people. Employees suggest they would like their jobs better if their boss would listen to them. Even when their superior asks them questions he sometimes interrupts their reply. Before they finish what they have to say, he gives them an answer to their half-stated idea or grievance.

Some managers suffer from compulsive talking. This blurs the true essence of dialogue with excessive verbiage. Real meaning becomes buried under a "heap-o'-words." Often, this indicates defensiveness on the part of the manager. Traditional diarrhea of words also indicates:

> The authoritarian manager
> A need for power and ego building
> Enjoyment at hearing one's own voice
> Insecurity (talking fills the silence)
> Disorganized thinking
> A lousy bad habit
> Desire to manipulate another person
> Existence of a parent-child relationship
> Frustration and a need to explode emotions

Through improved listening habits, a manager helps others and he helps himself. This is a list of benefits to the subordinate and to the manager, when the manager is a good listener

Subordinate	*Manager*
Hears his own problems	Focuses on problems and grievances
Releases hostilities, emotions	Gets thinking of the other person
Explores creative ideas	Develops understanding of others
Increases self-esteem	Engineers a climate for motivation
Understands his needs	Discovers another's needs
Establishes trust in his manager	Gains confidence and respect
Hears his own faults	Recognizes his own deficiencies
Gains self-understanding	Sees himself as others see him
Verbalizes thoughts and ideas	Seeks a solution
Motivates himself to action	Resolves a course of action

Listening to groups

Group discussions are being encouraged by managers as a means of surfacing problems shared by the entire group. The group serves a function that one-to-one dialogue doesn't. It affords a safety shelter for individuals. They feel secure with their peer relations. They'll speak out about issues they often wouldn't discuss with a manager on an individual basis. Needs of the group may be expressed by a leader or by several participants. Group numbers offer protection. We find that once a matter is put into the hopper by one member of a group, others feel free to speak. *The manager is now in a key position to listen to a consensus, therefore, he must listen!* The more he listens to, and is able to draw out of the group, the better his information regarding the total situation. By listening carefully, he has the opportunity with the group as a whole to either establish a rich rapport or to destroy respect. An important consideration: He must show appreciation for the others' ideas and feelings. He must make it known that he considers them as important as his own ideas and feelings. Although others' views may be opposite in nature to the concepts of the manager himself, he must acknowledge and respect them.

Categories of listeners

There are six general categories of listeners. These aren't distinct, definite lines of difference, but general categories into which people fall as listeners. Depending on circumstances, they may overlap or interchange.

1. *Total Listener:*

Concentrates on what's being said (doesn't shuffle papers on his desk, read, watch TV, etc.)

Listens to all the facts, not interrupting until the speaker has concluded his fact giving.

Listens for key words of interest on which to comment and ask questions.

Attempts to *understand* the *true meaning* of what's being said.

Is objective in trying to hear people as they actually are.

Holds back personal judgments until the speaker has presented his ideas.

Aims to hear the situation as a total picture, not as just a segment about which he wishes to intellectualize.

Reads feelings, emotions, and attitudes, not just words.

Feeds back for clarification and amplification.

Has as his objective a deeper understanding of the other person, his needs and problems.

2. *Tricky Listener:*

Appears to be totally engrossed in what's being said.

Can't wait to display his brilliance.

Listens attentively (outwardly only).

Hears only facts he can lift out of context to outwit, outsmart, and impress others.

Listens defensively.

Makes answers that are almost ALWAYS right, no matter what!

Impresses as listening with enthusiasm, but listens only to words, not to feelings.

3. *Intellectualized Listener:*

He's similar to the tricky listener, only he's more intent, more nonchalant, more convincing.

Employs logic to understand what's said, overlooks feelings.

Listens to only what he wants to hear.

Thinks solely in terms of what *he* will respond.

Hears only words, and ignores their intent.

Deals extensively with facts and statistics.

Ignores the impact his statements might have on the other person so long as he makes his point.

Wheels and deals in semantics.

Remains emotionally detached from the conversation.

Verbalizes in crisp, concise, and often cutting manner.

Retracts conversation skillfully, bringing it around to center on what *he* wants to talk about, or the point *he* wants to make.

4. *Superficial Listener:*

Engages in keeping things light, seldom talks anything of any substance.

Listens only to good things and ignores responses that are emotion packed.

Tunes out any provoking situations, ignoring response to such.

Judged a poor listener because he turns off to emotions and conflict.

Listens only to trivia and politeness, seldom to the gut-level nitty-gritty of everyday living.

Becomes a monologist; thus avoids having to listen when issues get heated.

Ignores personal issues, not wanting to understand nor to be understood by others.

Nods or shrugs shoulders rather than commit himself and become involved.

5. *Passive Listener:*

He's the extreme of the superficial listener. He's more cursory, more apt to be totally withdrawn from either listening or speaking.

Engages in superficial conversation only!

Looks right at the speaker—through him, is a poor listener.

Fears involvement either as a speaker or listener, believing that silence preserves peace.

Uses stock tie-offs: "I don't care." "Let's not talk about it." "Right." "That's all I have to say about the matter."

Hides his true feelings, keeping a tight mouth and closed ears. He's likely to explode violently someday.

Resents criticism, tranquility his only goal. Therefore, he won't listen to anything in depth.

Fears hearing facts so turns on TV, radio, or silence.

Retreats to solitary prison of his thoughts rather than let anyone into his world; won't listen for fear of becoming involved in weighty subjects dealing with life.

Employs aggressive conversationalist as a shield for his noninvolvement. He can just sit and not have to talk or listen.

Ignores any emotions, appearing to be totally insensitive to another's feelings.

6. *Never-Never Listener:*

Always speaking, he *can't be* a listener! He's the cocktail-party parrot, the compulsive chatterer, the seldom-listener, the office bore, and the feedback-jammer! He must be master of the conversation and always have the last word. Therefore, he's rarely interested in what anyone else has to say. Besides, he knows it all! What could anyone else tell him? So why should he listen?

Esprit de listening

What's the common spirit of listening that inspires enthusiasm in the conversation, and displays a strong regard for the other person's remarks? It's that vital part of virile dialogue, acknowledgement. It's a necessary courtesy, to acknowledge what you hear the other person saying, what his problem is, and then to ask him what he's doing to iron it out. First you must acknowledge having heard him and what he's said. In doing this you increase his self-esteem. You're listening to what he has to say. Actually, you pay him a high compliment in giving him your undivided attention. You tell him you value what he has to say, you respect his thinking, you appreciate him as a human being.

Acknowledgment is a primary indicator to another person to let him know you're listening. Say *something* even if it's in disagreement! If you don't acknowledge, the speaker doesn't know you're listening. As Cicero said, "For God's sake, disagree with me so that there can be two of us!" Disagreement is healthy and can make for a very lively and interesting exchange in dialogue.

Response on the part of the listener shouldn't always be in the form of a question. The posture of interrogation has its limitations in dialogue. Remember: Effective dialogue involves an exchange of ideas and feelings between two or more people. To exchange ideas, the listener can expand on what the other person has said. This expansion doesn't have to be an intellectualized dissertation. Sometimes short replies are more appropriate, just to let the person know you're listening. As an example: "What else?" "I understand." "How?" "I see." "Yes." "I believe you." "Then what happened?" "Why?" "I'm in agreement." Or, even the sound, "Hmmmmmm." *The spirit of listening is the acknowledgement of what's been said.*

In order to preserve conversation, even trivia should be acknowledged:

Two executives have just boarded their flight headed home after a business session.

Bert: I darned near got stuck in five o'clock traffic coming out here!

Elmer: Where's your report?

Elmer has just ignored Bert's conversation starter. Because of this, the conversation could continue like this.

Bert: I darned near got stuck in five o'clock traffic coming out here.

Elmer: Where's your report?

Bert: That damned bridge went up just as my cab approached it.

Elmer: I need the report to read while we're in flight.

Bert: They oughta do something about lifting the bridge during rush-hour traffic.

Elmer: I don't want to have to take the report home with me, etc.

Let's see how it goes when Elmer acknowledges Bert's remark:

Bert: I darned near got stuck in five o'clock traffic coming out here.

Elmer: The traffic's always lousy coming out at rush hour. Glad you made the flight. Say, I need to go over that report you have. I'd like to read it while we're in the air. How about sharing it with me now?

Bert: Sure, Elmer. I'll get it out of my briefcase, etc.

Simply by acknowledging each other's thoughts verbally, conversation can be sustained, grow, be exchanged. Disregarding conversation can be bad, but when the sender is confused by an unrelated reply it eventually ruins dialogue, diminishing it into two monologues. The exchange can also deteriorate into total silence or outraged anger over being ignored.

The great tune out, turn off:

The great tune out of conversation is when you turn off listening. Dialogue being a two-way street, when the receiver of words fails to respond, he turns off conversation, either diminishing it to a monologue or silence. The listener gets from listening in exact ratio to what he puts into it. If he listens intently he's apt to gain, but if he's just a hearer of sounds, he comes away from the encounter having been the recipient of sounds without meaning. The following incident depicts such a circumstance.

Case Study No. 28 / Right. Right. Right.

Cecil Anderson is the catalyst for a group of forty assembly-line workers. Most of them have worked under Ralph Long, the foreman, for his three and one-half years at this plant. Production has been decreasing steadily on the line, and Cecil, as spokesman for the group, is entering Ralph's office to discuss this with him.

Cecil: Hello, Boss. Got a minute I can talk with you?

Ralph: Right.

Cecil: Have you noticed recently the decrease in production?

Ralph: Right.

Cecil: I'm pretty concerned about this. Are you?

Ralph: Right.

Cecil: Would you like to know what some of the men are saying?

Ralph: Right.

Cecil: It's time for the cat to take a nap.

Ralph: Right.

Cecil: And the Eskimo's are building their igloos now.

Ralph: Right.

Cecil: Well, guess that's all I had to say. Goodby.

Ralph: Right. Come in to see me any time, Cecil. The door's always open.

Cecil: Right.

PROBLEM

Right? Right! Ralph hasn't heard a word Cecil has said. He isn't listening. Without participating fully in listening, it's impossible to hear what another says. It's also possible that important things won't be discussed because of this lack of listening.

ALTERNATE APPROACH

Cecil: Hello, Boss. Got a minute I can talk with you?

Ralph: Sure, Cecil. Come on in. Let's talk. What's buggin' you?

Cecil: That's what I came to see you about. I'm concerned about production on the line. Have you noticed, it's been on the decline for the past couple of months?

Ralph: Yes. I'm concerned, too, Cecil. You know the fellows better than I do. Can you pinpoint anything that might be causing this trouble?

Cecil: Yes. My grapevine has yielded several possible causes.

Ralph: OK. Let's put them on the table and see what we can do to get them cleared up.

EVALUATION

At this point Ralph and Cecil have become *involved* in conversation and can proceed to solving the problem. Why? Because Ralph LISTENED to and ACKNOWLEDGED *both* feelings and the verbal comments Cecil was communicating to him.

Causes of turn offs

1. *Psychological and sociological factors:* Due to the culture in which we live, we may be stimulated to avoid listening. Cultural mores, prejudices, stereotypes, taboos, preconceived ideas, and such

cause us to tune out dialogue. Then, there are psychological factors of a more personal nature, such as personal insecurity, attitudes, daily worries, fears, and hopes. All of these have direct bearing on what we listen to, and what we turn off.

2. *Audio factors:* Sounds other than those of dialogue are bound to have a distracting influence. Sometimes they cause us to turn away from the speaker as well as the noise, to turn off *all* sounds. Street noises, city sounds, children screaming, TV, radio, typewriters pounding, machines pulsating—all are audio distractions to listening.

3. *Visual factors:* In an office or at a meeting you can show people you aren't listening and this will jam the conversation channels. Some of these obvious distractions are clearing the desk, talking to someone else while another is speaking, doodling, not looking at the speaker, faking listening, fidgeting with some object, looking repeatedly and obviously at the clock, yawning and stretching, and so forth. These mannerisms can really turn off and tune out.

4. *Verbal factors:* Putting words into another person's mouth can cause them to stop listening:

    a. "You *don't care* about company policy!"

    b. "It seems *you just try to do* irritating things."

    c. "*All you want from me* is what I can produce in dollar volume!"

    d. "*The only time* I'm ever complimented is when you're going to criticize me."

    e. "You make big promises but *you never deliver!*"

The italicized words are the ones that stop the listening process. They, and others like them, are really telling the person what they're supposed to think. The same statements can be switched around to nurture conversation and keep listening alive:

    a. "What does company policy mean to you?"

    b. "I'm damned irritated by that last statement."

    c. "I get the feeling my only worth to the company is the dollar volume I produce, not the ideas I come up with."

    d. "I feel intimidated every time I get a compliment from you. I have the feeling I can expect a criticism next."

    e. "I'd like to see a higher rate of follow-through on these suggestions."

These statements in essence say the same things, but in a more powerful way. Most of them involve the speaker's feelings. They *do not tell* the listener what he's supposed to be doing, nor do they attack him directly. They tell him how the speaker feels. Since feelings govern and control words, it's more direct and stimulating to conversation to give your feelings. It's more meaningful than putting words into the other person's mouth.

5. *First-person-singular factor:* Another turn-off to listening is when "I" become so involved in what "I'm" saying and listening to "me," and thinking of what "I" want to say next, "I" fail to either see the other person's point of view or to respond to what he's said. When both parties involve in this sort of shut-out conversation, each person holds to his point of view. They don't hear the other person's point of view. The good things that are said are lost because no one is listening. This becomes intellectualized listening. We listen for only key words that allow us to intellectualize and respond. This is an advantageous form of listening when used in debate or formal discussion where intellect and reasoning are vital ingredients. In a one-to-one relationship, it's lethal. The purpose of daily conversation is to understand the person, not to display intellect. In a one-to-one relationship, it's more important to listen for attitudes and feelings than to listen to words that are being said. The following is a case in point:

Case Study No. 29 / I've Just About Had It!

Ryan Russell, a research chemist, has been an employee for six years, faithful, reliable, pleasant—a valuable employee. Hank Stanton is his boss. One day, immediately after lunch, Ryan confronts Hank in his office.

Ryan: I'm up to my ears right now, Hank!

Hank: Come in, sit down. What do you mean, Up to your ears?

Ryan: I don't want to sit down, and I mean I've just about had it! Today, Clark got the promotion I've been waiting for. I've waited three years now. I do the extra work around here and it's never even noticed. I put in extra time and it's never acknowledged. My ideas are implemented without acknowledgment. And now! I thought when this opening came along, I'd get the promotion. Instead Clark got it and I'm up-to-my-damned-ears-angry about it! You've got to be a yes-man around here and butter up to the big bosses like he did to get anywhere. No one notices me!

Hank: How do you know no one notices you?
Ryan: If they did, I'd have gotten the promotion!
Hank: What supervisors do you know who are yes-men?
Ryan: I can name a bunch of 'em!
Hank: What you say just isn't so. Forget about it!

PROBLEM

Hank is intellectualizing with Ryan. He's looking at the surface problem, and failing to listen for feelings—to understand Ryan's emotions and recognize them. With his intellectualization, Hank has closed the door to communications and to the possibility of understanding the problem as Ryan sees it.

ALTERNATE APPROACH

Ryan: I'm up to my ears right now, Hank!
Hank: Come in, Ryan, Come in, let's talk.
Ryan: I'm so damned mad right now, Hank, I could resign. I've just about had it!
Hank: Just about had it?
Ryan: Today, Clark got the promotion I've been waiting for. I've waited three years now. I do the extra work around here and it's never even noticed. I put in extra time and it's never acknowledged. My ideas are implemented without acknowledgment. And now! I thought when this opening came, I'd get the promotion. Instead, Clark got it and I'm up-to-my-damned-ears-angry about it! You've got to be a yes-man around here and butter up to the big bosses like he did to get anywhere. No one's noticed me!
Hank: You feel that your work hasn't been appreciated and recognized.
Ryan: That's right. All I ever get is a thank you from you when I do a good job.
Hank: The thank you doesn't satisfy your needs.
Ryan: Well, of course it does, up to a point. I appreciate your doing that, but I don't get any awards, or anything like that.
Hank: What you're saying is, you'd be happier with some public recognition of things you contribute that are just yours?
Ryan: Yes, like if I'd have gotten this promotion, people would have known I was good! That I was doing things right! I'd have gotten the title, "Supervisor of Research Chemists!" God, that sounds

good, Hank. SUPERVISOR OF RESEARCH CHEMISTS! I've thought about having new business cards printed up with my name and *that* on them.

Hank: The title would have made you feel good.

Ryan: Oh, man! You just don't know! I'd be on cloud nine with that! But, what happened? Clark got it and I'm still in the bull pen of research chemists!

I saw him at lunch the other day with the top brass. When I saw that, I knew he was buttering them up, or something was happening there. All at once, I didn't see my new business cards in front of me any more. I saw Clark's instead.

Hank: I hear lots of disappointment in that statement, Ryan.

Ryan: Disappointment? Damned right. And I don't know what I'll tell my wife. She thought I'd get the promotion, too.

Hank: Now that I understand your feelings, I'd like to give the matter further consideration. The situation with Clark will have to be maintained. But I have some ideas. I can't commit myself now, but there are areas I can take a closer look at. Will you get back to me tomorrow afternoon? Three is open on my calendar.

Ryan: Sure, Hank, sure! I appreciate your consideration. See you at three.

EVALUATION

Because Hank recognized Ryan's feelings, he now understands his problem and has more comprehensive knowledge of Ryan's motivations. Now he has the necessary information with which to seek a solution and take action.

It may be relatively simple to save a reliable employee like Ryan. In this instance, to satisfy Ryan's motivation, Hank could (a) establish another title such as technical vice-president or technical supervisor, etc.; (b) establish an award of the month for public recognition of people like Ryan; or (c) award achievement pins, etc. Any of these courses of action would help to satisfy the ego needs Ryan has displayed.

If Ryan has these needs unsatisfied, it would be a strong indication there are others in this company who could benefit by some public recognition of their endeavors.

6. *Advice-giving factor:* As the listener, when we become the advice giver, we're apt to get turned off. Giving advice is a great ego

booster for the self-imagined psychiatrist. His ego is boosted that someone has verbalized a problem to him and asked for his advice. Advice is cheap, and seldom listened to or acted upon. Most of us who have a problem take action on *only* the solution that *we* resolve. Talking out the problem is helpful in finding a path of action. That's why it's vitally important for you to listen.

Erich Fromm sums it up well:

> To be concentrated in relation to others means primarily to be able to listen. Most people listen to others, or even give advice, without really listening. They do not take the other person's talk seriously, they do not take their own answers seriously either. As a result, the talk makes them tired. They are under the illusion that they would be even more tired if they listened with concentration. But the opposite is true. Any activity, if done in concentrated fashion, makes one more awake, while every unconcentrated activity makes one sleepy. . . .[25]

To keep conversation in tune, we need to put our energies to thinking constructively and listening constructively rather than defensively.

7. *Human factors:* Another incident that can shut down our listening plant is when we become distracted by what we see. When a good-looking woman catches your eye, no matter how brilliant the conversation, the old axiom holds true, "A picture is worth a thousand words!" And with that picture, words can't compete!

To stay tuned in

To be a good listener we must discipline ourselves to listen to what's being said verbally and nonverbally. We must shut out as much as possible, our personal interpretations of the context of what's being said. This means listening to the situation as it exists, not listening as we'd like it to be (future) or listening in the past (as it has been), but listening in the present tense of here and now!

Listening takes courage. What we hear might upset us! It might cause us to think, to become involved with the attitudes and ideas of others. It could mean we'd have to change some of our own attitudes and ideas, to re-align some of our thinking. It takes courage to listen to someone speak. It takes courage to put aside our own selfish needs and devote ourselves to another. Only through such concern in listening can we come to know ourselves and to share with others. Listening means we might be stirred to change, to improve, to grow, and to learn.

To be a total listener requires a high degree of cultivated concentration. Again quoting from Erich Fromm: "To be concentrated means to live fully in the present, in the here and now, and not to think of the next thing to be done, while I am doing something right now."[26]

Let's show curiosity and enthusiasm to the speaker. Let's be alive and receptive to him, centering our total attention and interests on him and what he's saying.

LISTENING DEVICES

Feedback

To avoid jaded understanding of what is being said in dialogue, FEED BACK! This means to feed back a reaction to what's been said. This may or may not be a question. It might take the form of a statement that acknowledges agreement or re-states, in our words, the person's remarks in capsule form. The purpose of feedback is to check for verification or clarification of images and words that have just been spoken. This isn't done for every statement made. It's used as a summary or recap at various intervals during conversation or when specific statements are without clear meaning. *You want to be sure you're both talking about the same thing.* You can gain better insight into another's point of view, his attitudes and feelings, through feedback. It must flow freely and frankly if it's to have value for the participants. Feedback serves two purposes: It provides information about the other person, and it provides us with information about ourselves.

It's possible to modify our point of view more readily when we receive feedback from an outside source. We may be unaware of our feelings or point of view until we verbalize it and it's fed back to us through another's words. Hearing someone else paraphrase what we say is often the only way we can hear ourselves.

What are the advantages of feedback in listening?

1. It assures the other person that you got the true meaning of his statement.

2. It's preventative in nature, helping to avoid argument and mis-interpretation.

3. It's like a tape being played back to the other person when he hears someone else saying what he's just said.

4. Ideas can be aired for mutual understanding. They can be evaluated more rationally.

5. It avoids the "can-you-top-this" syndrome.

6. Major points can be clarified. It keeps in focus the major subject.

7. It prevents openly rejecting an idea and perserves a neutral attitude.

We need feedback to be sure we hear things correctly. Many things can influence our hearing at a given moment. A different time and a different place when the same subject is under discussion, and we might see things differently. If we're feeling tired, happy, exhilarated, frustrated—whatever we're feeling will influence the quality of our listening. What technical and factual knowledge we possess is an influence. We're influenced by what pressures are being currently exerted on us by our needs—family, job, community, financial. All of these elements determine how we receive words at a given time. This is why we must have feedback to be sure that we understand what's being said.

When we receive criticism, our emotions don't permit us to hear clearly. Generally we hear only what we want to hear. When we feed back the major points of criticism we're more apt to understand, first, what they are, second, why the points have been made, and third, the circumstances that caused the criticism to be leveled against us. When a manager doesn't agree totally with facts offered him, he tends to ignore them. Next time the facts won't be offered. Hearing isn't always agreeing. We must acknowledge facts that are presented. One way to feed back on this is to say, "What I hear you saying is. . . . I respect your right to your opinion. However, I can't agree with you." Although you aren't in agreement, you have fed back for acknowledgment and clarification. You've stated your point of respecting his right to his ideas. Occasionally we can't agree because of a lack of understanding. Re-statement makes this apparent for us.

Through feedback the manager demonstrates:

1. An interest for the other person, his feelings, attitudes, ideas.

2. An objective attitude on his part.

3. He's listening to what's been said, not just thinking of what he wants to say.

4. A sincerity and genuine concern for the other person.

The manager must get feedback to know if he's being heard.

The best way to drive people away is to not listen. When one person presents an idea or asks a question and the other person doesn't respond, there's no real impregnation of the idea.

The following situation evidences both of these factors: lack of feedback and turn off of listening.

Case Study No. 30 / People-Repellent

Chris Evans is production manager in a frozen-food plant. He's just been called into the office of his immediate supervisor, Randy Johnson.

Randy: Can you tell me, Chris, what you think is causing the turnover of key people in your department?

Chris: I'm not really sure.

Randy: Don't be evasive. What's at the bottom of this turnover?

Chris: I don't know.

Randy: Then who does know?

Chris: I don't know. I can't help you.

Randy: Something's at the bottom of this and I'm going to find out what it is!

PROBLEM

Randy has alienated Chris with his threatening attack-method. He became parent with his admonition, "Don't be evasive." Chris became defensive and the conversation stalemated.

ALTERNATE APPROACH

Randy: Chris, I have a need and I think you can help me with it.

Chris: Let's hear it, Randy.

Randy: There's a high rate of turnover in your department the last six months. I need to know what's causing this. Can you help me?

Chris: I'm not really sure.

Randy: You're saying you know something that could be the cause.

Chris: I've been trying to figure it out myself. I've talked with the catalyst and others. No one is saying anything. Instead, they're just walking—right out of their jobs!

Randy: We both know we can't stand this kind of turnover much longer. It's not only the dollar cost, but it's gotten to the point it's difficult to find competent skilled personnel.

Chris: What you're saying is, we've reached the end of the rope.

Randy: Right!

Chris: I'm going to quit playing games with you, Randy. I know damned good and well why the key people are pulling out.

Brace yourself. It's because of the young pip-squeak of a son-o'-the president! He's been here eight months now. He alienates the whole crew. He's like a killer dog turned loose in a herd of sheep!

Randy: What you re telling me is that we have one person who's doing all the damage?

Chris: That's my thinking, Randy. That's why no one will make any clear statement on their exit interviews. They won't say why they're quitting. I'm ready to quit myself. Every time I see him coming toward me, I'm just like the others, I cringe. He must spray himself with "people-repellent" every morning!

Randy: What's your feeling about confronting him?

Chris: I shudder and quake! But, he's under my wing—and in my hair. I suppose I'll have to do something about it.

Randy: You're reluctant to confront him.

Chris: Reluctant! Damned right! Wouldn't you be, too? He's the boss' favorite son, in training to replace daddy! How did I get so lucky, having him assigned to me?

Randy: Can you propose a course of action?

Chris: I'll face him and have it out with him today. It's putting my head on the block, but it's either that or quit myself. One way I may get fired—the other way, I may quit. But if I don't talk to him, dozens of others *will quit.* It's an intolerable situation as it stands. So, lucky Chris goes forth to confront the president's son.

Randy: You'll talk with him today.

Chris: This afternoon. You can count on me to let you know the outcome. Or, if you don't hear from me, just send flowers!

Randy: Good luck, Chris.

EVALUATION

Randy approached Chris, asking for his help (not demanding it). Although Chris was reluctant to level with Randy, when he did, the problem surfaced. There was good listening and feedback on the part of both Randy and Chris. Without both of these elements working dialogical understanding becomes nonexistent.

Listening for feelings

Words can be diametrically opposed to thoughts and feelings. We say one thing—we mean another. Emotions and feelings control what's said. When one's in a high state of exhilaration and says, "That's great!" we immediately read the underlying feelings of enthusiasm and agreement; the words and feelings are saying the same thing. Take the same statement when a person is disgusted with a proposal and says, "That's great," and we read the emotion of disinterest or disagreement. In this second instance the feelings were diametrically opposed to what the words said. It's essential to total listening to listen for thoughts and feelings, not just to words. Listening for feelings is another listening device. By doing this we're better able to realize the implied meanings behind words. Then we can focus on truthful meanings to establish better rapport.

Feelings are the basis of communication. They affect our interpretation of what's said. In order to relate to others we must involve ourselves in a process of freeing ourselves of words *per se.* We must sharpen our sensitivity to the feelings and emotions of others, respecting these feelings and sharing these emotions.

Listening with our eyes

We act out physically what we believe and what we feel. "Your actions speak so loudly, I can't hear what you say." Psychology takes the stand that an individual reflects the inner person in what he does more than by what he says. Human behavior is the outward expression of inner attitudes, needs, and thinking. Our physical being mirrors our mind. Therefore, we must observe others visually to understand them better. Another listening device, our eyes.

As infants before we could talk, we communicated our feelings with body movements. If we were happy we smiled and cooed, if angry we shook our clenched fist and kicked our feet and cried. We do the same as adults, in a more suppressed, "sophisticated" manner. When we feel good we laugh, smile, are pleased, and our bodies are relaxed. But if we're frustrated by something we'll clench our fists, walk with a heavy step, and scowl with our face. These are feelings being demonstrated through our bodily gestures. They're just a few of the ways in which our body English speaks. Observing this, we learn much of the inner person and what's going on within their thinking at any given moment.

Word choice

Another listening device for us is the choice of words themselves. If someone transmits, "I don't know," that can say, "I don't have the knowledge with which to reply," or it can say, "I'm undecided." As a listener, giving feedback will clarify such indefinite terms as "I don't know." When a person transmits, "It's OK," he may be giving approval with reservation. But if he says, "I'm in total agreement," his choice of words tells us there's no reservation, but total agreement. Words mean different things to different people. As a listener, it's important to understand the meaning the sender implies in his choice of words.

Tones, rhythm, tempo

Tones, rhythm, and tempo of speech will indicate feelings for the listener. They can be instant guidelines for the "temperature" of the encounter at that particular moment. This is tones, rhythm, and tempo in dialogue:

"*I* don't care what you do" = I *personally* don't care.
"I *don't* care what you do" = I really *don't* care.
"I don't *care* what you do" = Do damned well as you please.
"I don't care *what* you do" = You have free reign, do as you wish.
"I don't care what *you* do" = I don't care what you do, but I care what others do.
"I don't care what you *do*" = It's what you don't do that bugs me.
"*I don't care what you do*" = Just get the hell out of my office!

In reading words we must cultivate the habit of analyzing the motive behind the words. These three questions will be helpful in our analysis. "What does he mean besides what he's saying?" "How does he feel?" And, "What does he want?" These are questions that our subconscious should be asking when we're listening to another. How do we find the answers to these questions? We listen for tones of voice, choice of words, and the rhythm and tempo of their presentation. In addition, we watch the other person for body English. The combination of physical gestures and verbalization will amplify understanding of what the communicator is really trying to get across to us. We must use all our listening devices to allow our cybernetics of dialogue to perform at peak efficiency.

FOCUS ON PROBLEMS

Problems exist in everyday life. Trite as that statement may seem, there are people who don't want to admit the existence of problems. They procrastinate acknowledging them or doing anything about them. But, problems don't just dissolve. They're there and will stay and multiply unless, and until, we face them and seek their solutions. Problems exist in individuals and within situations.

It's necessary for the manager—to be effective in his job—to be aware of his own problems, those of his subordinates, and the problems involved in his work environment. Through his awareness of these problems, he can work toward solutions. Otherwise, he's incapable of implementing change. How then, can the manager locate problem areas—how can he focus on the problem? To discover the problem itself, its cause, and to reach a workable solution, we must dialogue. Then we're able to establish a path for action. Unless we're aware of our own problems and those of the people with whom we work, it's difficult to understand either ourselves or our co-workers, to improve when we don't know what needs improving, to grow when we don't know what needs changing.

Robert E. Moore, in *The Human Side of Successful Communication*,[27] reports the results of a survey done by a team of University of Michigan psychologists, among top-level businessmen in manufacturing, oil, and utility companies,

> . . . and they found that the boss seldom knew what his junior executive's problems were. Frequently the two men did not even agree on what the subordinate was supposed to be doing!

In only 6 percent of the cases were the two men in complete agreement about the junior executive's problems. In 20 percent of the cases there was some agreement. In 74 percent of the cases there was practically no agreement about the areas of trouble.

Isn't this rather amazing evidence of communication failure among management people whose positions would indicate that they are above average in intelligence and education!

"How can I change if I don't know what's wrong with me?" Unless we become aware of our faults, it's difficult for us to do anything about them. Whether we're speaking as individuals, or as a company, it's of extreme importance to us to know our faults, and problems. Otherwise, how can we change for the better? How can we improve our products? How can we improve our relations with other human beings? How can we change ourselves?

Carlyle sums it up: "The greatest of faults, I should say is to be conscious of none."

A customer doesn't buy our product because something doesn't meet his need. He fails to complain about it—he just doesn't buy OUR product. The same thing may be true with an employee. He doesn't tell us of some of our faults. He reacts in the same way the customer did—he just tunes us out. It's difficult to improve our product or ourselves if we don't know what's wrong with us.

Criticism

Most managers aren't too comfortable when it comes to criticizing an employee. It's difficult when we have to reprimand a subordinate, but if we're to focus on the problem and help him to improve, isn't this part of our job? When suggesting criticism, we should keep in mind it's of prime importance for us to criticize the *problem* and not the person.

Any time criticism is leveled, it should be directed toward the act itself, not to the individual. If you're playing football, which of these three criticisms would you prefer hearing the coach yell to you from the sidelines?

"You dumb meat-head! You fumbled the ball!"

"You're back too far!"

"Get *under* the ball!"

Either the second or third would be more acceptable than the first.

Rational: The first attacked the player himself as a person (meathead). The second and third suggested how the *play* was wrong, or how it could have been corrected. By criticizing the *act* rather than the person, you preserve the person's self-esteem. On attacking the problem, through dialogue, you can help impart information, facts, judgments, experience, counseling, and perhaps a sharing experience.

Dialogue is a more amenable way to criticize the act, rather than the person himself. Through dialogue, it's easier for both parties to give their point of view. There may be a valid reason for his action (or yours) or the lack thereof. Through dialogue, criticism becomes more comfortable, more tolerable. It also allows for asking rather than telling. You can *ask* the person to pinpoint what *he thinks* the problem is, rather than telling him what *you think* it is. There's a difference. When you *ask his thinking*, it's adult to adult. When you *tell* him, it's parent telling child.

The following incident will point up this difference:

Case Study No. 31 / Job Fatigue

Andy Tully is supervisor in an automobile-parts manufacturing plant. He's noticed a problem with Red Davis, and calls to him as he passes Red's bench.

Andy: What the heck are you up to, Red! You're doing a lousy job lately. You'd better shake it up to meet rate today or you're on the block! Let's get with it!

Red: (To his partner about Andy) *You* can get without it, you dumb bastard! I don't have to take that kind of crap from anyone, not even you. I'm gonna foul up that Vaseline record of yours today. I'll put so much sand in it, it'll look like the bottom of the ocean. Then we'll see who'll get shaken up!

PROBLEM

Should Andy have reprimanded his subordinate in the presence of his co-workers? To belittle him was to demean him in the eyes of his peers. Andy attacked the person, not the act. This made Red look small to his co-workers, and deflated his personal esteem. Andy didn't focus on the problem: *what* was "lousy" about Red's performance. He's incurred Red's anger, and it's fair to conjecture Red will carry out his threat. Had Andy respected him as a human being, his response might have been less vitriolic.

ALTERNATE APPROACH

Andy asks Red to join him in his office.

Andy: How have things been going lately, Red?

Red: OK, I guess. I'm waiting for vacation.

Andy: For vacation?

Red: Yeh, I know it's almost three months away, but I'm looking forward to it.

Andy: Why do you look so far ahead, Red?

Red: I've been awful tired lately. I don't know what's wrong. I'm just tired. Guess it's time for me to go fishin' and rest up.

Andy: Is there any particular reason *why* you're tired?

Red: No, not that I think of. Everything's OK.

Andy: I've noticed recently your production is down some. Do you suppose the tiredness has anything to do with that?

Red: Well, yeh, I guess it has. I think maybe I'm tired of what I've been doing. You know I've been here for three years now. I've done the same job since I came here. Guess it's kinda monotonous.

I figured it out the other day. Just to make rate, I turn 2,124 screws in that same piece of equipment every day. Let's say I work 250 days a year. That means in three years I've turned a total of 1,593,000 screws. Now, no matter how you look at it, that's one hell of a lot of turning!

Andy: You'd like to do something else.

Red: I guess so. It's really an easy job, and there are lots of guys who would like doing it. I did, too, for awhile. But after three years, 2,124 times a day—well, I guess anyone would get bored.

Andy: I should have recognized that myself, Red. You were so efficient, I didn't think you were bored.

Let's get you transferred to another machine for awhile. When you learn another operation, we'll interchange you between that and your present job. It'll help to relieve your boredom. I think it might even get rid of some of your fatigue.

Red: I'd like to try it. I think switching jobs, I'll do better. Then I can keep up rate for you. I hate to let you down. I know it means money to you when I do. It's just that I've been so tired.

Andy: I know that, Red. We'll take one thing at a time and see how it goes from there.

Red: Thanks, Boss.

EVALUATION

Andy may have uncovered the possible cause of Red's production loss, job fatigue. He directed the conversation to focus the dialogue on the problem. When Andy encouraged Red to tell his story, adult to adult, it didn't come off sounding like criticism. It was more easy and comfortable for both compared to the first encounter when Andy attacked Red before his peers. When he railed out at Red, he was acting as a parent scolding a child in front of his playmates. In essence, complaints and criticism are more easily handled and less painful, when dialogue is used to uncover the problems and participants then proceed to seek solutions.

Another way of explaining the first situation of Andy and Red is to quote Dr. Rensis Likert, former director of the University of Michigan Institute for Social Research, on a study which was done involving several thousand employees and their supervisors:

> Those supervisors whose units have a relatively poor production record tend to concentrate on keeping their subordinates busily engaged in going through a specific work cycle in a prescribed way and at a satisfactory rate as determined by time standards. . . Supervisors with the best records of performance focus their primary attention on the human aspects of their subordinates' problems and on endeavoring to build effective work groups with high performance goals.[28]

Constructive criticism produces understanding and growth about things that are in need of change. Invalid criticism accomplishes nothing but ill will and usually passive resistance, as we saw in the first encounter in the case of *Job Fatigue*. If an invalid criticism is leveled at you, challenge its validity. It's unnecessary to be tyrannized by the compulsive carper. Express your thinking about the objection. If it's irrelevant or invalid, pursuing it can only be a waste of time and energy. But, if it *is* valid, admit it. Proceed to work it out.

There are two major areas of thinking regarding how criticism should be given. The first says we should always compliment before criticizing. The second contends that, if we do that, eventually every time we compliment someone they'll have a conditioned response of "OK, what have I done wrong?"

Focus on the problem immediately, stating clearly what we see the problem to be. This appears to be a more honest beginning. Get it on the table, then find something to compliment. People can be resentful when they're disarmed by a compliment, then shot down by a blast of critical buckshot! An individual can retaliate with a vengeance to that type of trickery, and we can destroy our credibility doing this. Better to focus on the problem first. State it, clear the air, seek the solution, then compliment.

Although it isn't thought of as part of the job to offer constructive criticism to a superior, if we're really a friend shouldn't we do just that? If not, why not?

There are three paramount reasons for our failure to focus on a superior's weakness *in his presence:*

1. We fear being aggressive with someone who is our superior. We don't want to incur his wrath, or his disfavor.

2. If we zing him, we're leaving ourselves wide open for him to zing us back. We feel more vulnerable to his retaliation to our actions.

3. What if he fires us? Job loss is probably the greatest fear as to "why not?"

All of these are FEARS. They're based on the preconceived, preconditioned, structured sociological relationship that's supposed to exist between superior and subordinate.

Can we think of these things not as FEARS, but as RISKS? They're fears only as they exist in the individual's mind. To tell your superior how you really feel involves a risk, but wouldn't that be an easier way of working with him than to live with your feelings all inside of you? Either way there's bound to be an indication of turbulence in the relationship. One is turbulence of short duration (take the chance and tell him), the other is of endless duration (when you decide never to tell him, but live with it inside you).

To be considered: When you're enjoying a good, healthy working relationship with your superior and you offer criticism that's valid, there's a good chance it'll be understood and accepted as such. If the relationship is so strained you don't feel you have the right to contribute your suggestions, then the relationship is in danger, anyway. Consider a move to a job where you'll work with a manager with whom you could be more comfortable.

A person can't change and rectify his faults and errors if he's both threatened and unaware of the faults and errors. Usually we're so close to our faults we can't be objective. Literally, we're unable to see our own mistakes and certainly not in the same perspective others see them. People do us no favor by *not* leveling with us about our mistakes. *We cannot change unless we know what needs changing*, and have a constructive climate in which we strive to change.

The following case points up the need for having another tell us our faults—to criticize—and most important, to get down to the *real problem*. Trivia has no place here.

Case Study No. 32 / "Who, Me?"

Wayne Kent is vice-president of a large midwest milling company. He's an employee of twenty-one years who has worked his way up the company ladder. He's loyal, dedicated, a "company man."

Paul Sawyer is Wayne's superior and they've been friends for many years. The past four or five years, Paul has noticed an increasing amount of absenteeism and tardiness on Wayne's part. As far as Paul can discern, the cause for this is excessive drinking.

Last week, Wayne completely missed an important board meeting in New York. He's made no mention of this. Paul now is faced with confronting Wayne with his problem of absenteeism and tardiness.

The setting is the executive suite in the home office.

Paul: Hello, Wayne, back from the trip?

Wayne: Yes, travel sure isn't what it used to be. It's no fun any more. Just a hassel with airlines and hotels and bars, and people to be entertained.

Paul: Yes, it isn't like the good old days. And, speaking of the good old days, Wayne, I've been looking at some of your activities for the past several months. I notice you've been missing lots of time from the office and from meetings. Were you aware of this?

Wayne: Oh, not really. I think there were a few times when my plane's been late and I've gotten to the office after my usual time.

Paul: Maybe, but it isn't the occasional miss I'm talking about. There seems to be a real strong and frequent pattern of absenteeism and tardiness.

Wayne: I think you're imagining things, Paul. You've always been a mother hen.

Paul: Well, I think it's something to be watched in the future. You're a valuable man, and we need your time on the job.

Wayne: Look, I've worked my way up from the bottom, Paul. I couldn't have done that if I'd been goofing along the way.

Paul: True, Wayne. True. Well, I guess I'd better get back to my office. Take it easy.

Wayne: Sure, Paul. You, too.

PROBLEM

Is Paul focusing on the *real* problem? He mentioned only the obvious problem, the symptomatic problem, that of absenteeism and tardiness, but he didn't mention the area of drinking or the important board meeting. Wayne is sidestepping the issue, too. Neither is being direct about what the major issue is—Wayne's drinking problem.

Admittedly, this is a touchy issue to discuss. But because it hasn't been brought into the open, there's little chance for Wayne to know how Paul feels about it.

ALTERNATE APPROACH

Paul: Hello, Wayne, back from the trip?

Wayne: Yes, travel sure isn't what it used to be. It's no fun any more. Just a hassle with airlines and hotels and bars, and people to be entertained.

Paul: Speaking of things not being what they used to be, Wayne, I've been noticing some of your activities of the past several months. I have to level with you. Some of the officers and I are concerned about you.

You've been absent from lots of things and tardy to more. You *missed* the board meeting of the year last week in New York, and you haven't even mentioned it. Can you tell me what you think is causing your lack of job performance, especially the lack of attendance?

Wayne: I really wasn't aware that I wasn't meeting the performance expected of me.

Paul: Then what you're telling me is, you don't see any indications of a problem relating to your job?

Wayne: That's right, Paul.

Paul: Then I've got to give you my thinking about the cause of your absenteeism and tardness. I feel the problem may be a result of your drinking.

Wayne: You're crazy, Paul. I drink a little every day, that's true, but I'm no alcoholic!

Paul: I didn't say that you're an alcoholic. I said I think you may have a *problem* with your drinking.

Wayne: I've just overslept a few times and missed a couple of planes. But I don't have a drinking problem.

Paul: Only you can know that, Wayne. And I respect your judgment. I must make my position clear, though. I respect your right to drink where you want, when you want, with whom you want, and in whatever quantity you want, *as long as it doesn't interfere with your job.*

I have to repeat that last part of the statement again: *as long as it doesn't interfere with your job.* Here's what makes me feel there's a problem. Missing meetings, days out of the office, and taking all-afternoon lunch hours are, in my book, an infringement on your job time and performance.

Wayne: You sure make your point clear, Paul. I had no idea I'd been missing time. You know I love this company more than anything. I don't want to jeopardize my position here. But I don't have a problem with drinking.

Paul: Only *you* can make that decision, Wayne. I respect your right to spend your time outside of business as you choose. But I also must ask when it comes to the job that you're here, and in condition to conduct your part of the business.

Wayne: OK, Paul. I think I get the message. What do you want me to do?

Paul: It isn't what *I* want you to do, Wayne. It's what *you* want to do. It's your decision to make, how you want to conduct your life. It's my responsibility to see to it that your working time is spent productively. You know my thinking. And if I can help you in any way, let's talk about it. Let's meet again, one month from today, here, and see how things look then. This company needs your intelligence and experience, Wayne. We want your full cooperation to help us to continue to be a growing, successful company.

Wayne: What can I say right now, Paul, except thanks for leveling with me? I think I can handle things now.

EVALUATION

Wayne's feelings were recognized and his rights were acknowledged. Paul told him exactly where he and the company stood on such matters. He was tactful in not calling Wayne an alcoholic, and in not telling him that he had to quit drinking, etc. Paul's approach embodied elements of candor and tact; both are necessary ingredients in handling a personal matter such as problem drinking.

The following is a statement regarding management's role in the handling of alcoholism, by Ross Von Wiegland, Director of Labor-Management Services, National Council on Alcoholism, Inc., New York:

> It is a fact industry has the best motivational tool known to date for motivating a problem drinker to accept treatment. The employed alcoholic desires to hold his job.
>
> Early detection of the problem drinker is noticeable in his job performance and his related behavior patterns. It will evidence itself here long before it is noticed in physical manifestations. It is industry's challenge to discover the potential alcoholic before others would detect him. By documenting unsatisfactory job performance, the supervisor can catch the symptoms at their earliest stages. At this point, an interview with the potential problem drinker, pointing out his job performance record, serves as a warning to him. His alternatives would be a decrease in salary, demotion, etc., or confidential treatment and consultation to aid him in rehabilitation to continue his present position. Recovery rates on this procedure are documented: For every one-hundred persons who receive early confidential treatment, two out of three recover.
>
> The U.S. Department of Health, Education, and Welfare estimates that alcoholism costs industry *two billion dollars annually.* It pays industry to create a climate for motivation to aid the problem drinkers to get help. Managers are in the best position to be early detectors by noticing changes in employee job performance.

In management, the goal isn't to change people, but to change what they do. This can best be done through a direct focus on their problems, and an attempt to motivate them to want to change themselves.

Again, you cannot change any other person. Only you can change yourself. Only he can change himself.

A gripe not aired can become a grudge

Emotional cancer can be the result of gripes that aren't aired. When people hold inside them their dislikes and problems, it can become an explosive thing and the real problems become lost in the emotions. Explosions can be avoided by letting off steam before it gets to that point. One way to do this is to make an appointment to dialogue about whatever it is that's bothering you. The more objectively, calmly, and deliberately you can organize your thinking, the better. This is the purpose of making the appointment rather than just blasting in and firing away with temper and confusion.

When you make the appointment, it's well to state why you want to see the person. Mention that you would like to talk about a specific issue. This can save verbal wandering. It's also fairer to the other person as it doesn't keep him dangling, wondering why you want to see him.

Mutually favored times are rare, but postponement can be dangerous. Make the appointment, even if it's for a couple of days later. You may be surprised to discover how tensions will ease when the appointment has been made. This also allows for a cooling-off period during which the original violence of the gripe may dwindle.

Meaningful results in interpersonal communications and dialogue come when employer and employee get together and have it out. Sometimes this is politely referred to as "negotiating." *If there isn't confrontation, then there isn't growth.*

It's unwise to do the other person's thinking for him. Yet, if we don't have it out, this is what we end up doing.

Discuss the problem, get his thinking. You'll never know how he really feels about something unless you ask him.

In close relation to doing someone's thinking for him, is the "Cyrano syndrome." This is when you ask someone else to do your talking for you. Face it yourself, say it yourself! Otherwise, it may never be said. Or, if it is said by another, the interpretation may not be as you intended. It can become distorted, or not presented factually, and it may even be said so it's damaging to you. If you have a problem, confront the person whom it involves *yourself* and "speak for yourself, John."

Underlying meaning

Is the stated problem always the real problem? As we've seen, often the most obvious elements in a problem are at best symptoms of the real problem. When we don't air our tensions, we build them within ourselves as our own little world of anxieties and the slightest thing can trigger our tempers. We explode about an irrelevancy, something that has no bearing on what's really disturbing us. When you don't feel good toward someone, or about an incident, even the tock of the clock can set off your emotions. It's important, therefore, to focus on the real problem. Avoid argument and instead dialogue about things that are germane to the real issue.

The case of *I've Got to Leave* illustrates someone stating one thing as the problem and meaning another:

Case Study No. 33 / I've Got to Leave!

Van Ford has worked with a restaurant chain for eighteen years, starting as a busboy. He has worked his way up and now heads their high-volume catering department. This promotion necessitated his moving from the East to the Midwest. His qualifications were unquestionable, and his zest for this new position was satisfying to both him and his superior.

One Thursday morning, he rushed into the office of his superior, Chad Carson, and said:

Van: It's all over. I quit! I can't take it any longer. I'm going to leave!

Chad: What's this all about, Van?

Van: I don't like it here. It was a mistake for me to move here. I was beautifully comfortable back East. This city isn't for me!

Chad: I thought you liked your new position, Van.

Van: It isn't that, Chad, it isn't that at all. I just have to ask for a transfer back to the East.

Chad: I can't do much about that, if that's your decision. I'll see what I can do to get you back there.

PROBLEM

Why is Van really quitting? Why does he want to transfer? Chad is being passive to accept Van's resignation from his employ without any further inquiry as to why.

ALTERNATE APPROACH

Van: It's all over. I quit! I can't take it any longer. I'm going to leave!

Chad: You can't take it any longer?

Van: That's right. This is about the most stupid thing I ever did.

Chad: What's stupid, Van?

Van: Moving here to the Midwest. It isn't working out.

Chad: Are you saying the job isn't working out?

Van: No, anything but that. You know I like my new job. The challenge is great, but I can't see any other way than to move back East.

Chad: Can you tell me what's at the bottom of this?

Van: It's my family. I didn't think they'd take it this way. They haven't been able to adjust here. The only solution is to go back East where they have their friends and are established.

Chad: I respect your decision to go back, Van, if that's the way it has to be. But, let's see if there's something we can do to help get this thing straightened out.

You've been here for about six weeks now? I haven't done my part to help you get settled. What about you and your wife coming out to the country club with Katherine and me this Saturday? Let's get you involved in some local social life.

Van: Maybe that'd help. Let me talk to my wife about it. I'll admit, we haven't gotten involved in *anything* socially so far.

Chad: Sorry I've neglected getting you into these activities. Let's see about memberships for you. That'd help provide activities for the kids, too. Let me know what their interests are. I'll see what I can uncover that would be valuable for them.

Van: That sounds like a good beginning. I've been so busy on the job, getting it set up to operate with the new guidelines. You know I've been working twelve and fourteen hours a day. Because of this, I guess, I've neglected the family.

Chad: Let's do something about that, too. Why don't you take long weekends for the next month? If we re-arrange schedules and plan ahead, it should be no problem. If that'll help, maybe we can change schedules between us so we can alternate long weekends.

Van: That would be great. It would sure make Fran and the kids happy. There's been lots of tension with the move. If we can plan some family activity, it'll take the edge off things.

Chad: Let's try these for openers, Van, and see how we do. I'll be interested to know Fran's reaction—and the kids', too. When they're not happy, I know you aren't. You can count on me for support.

Van: Thanks. I feel better myself. I have an idea the family will share my relief. It's worth a try. I don't want to move again. I don't think they do either. We'll give it a try.

EVALUATION

Much of the tension seems to have been relieved because Chad uncovered the real "why" Van "couldn't stand it any longer." He recognizes the fact that tensions at home can cause tensions on the job. Subsequently, he moved to aid Van in relieving the problems at home as much as he could.

Although it isn't always possible to discover the real cause for a problem, it's only right to look for it.

Person-to-person communications is the optimum way to seek out and pinpoint problem areas. These may be negative in form or positive.

Negative problems are production lag, inferior attitudes, marketing target-procedures, and so on. Positive problem areas are those dealing with a need to compliment people, to motivate them through acknowledging good attitudes, promotions, company success, and so forth. If these positive things are not verbalized, they can erode into negative problems. Herzberg defines these as some of the hygiene factors. They seem irrelevant, and they are until they're neglected and become full-blown problems.

The manager develops self-confidence when he faces a problem and solves it. Mistakes are inevitable and mistakes within reason mean growth. But first there must be an awareness of them as we will discover in the instance of Norman and Pat:

Case Study No. 34 / Decrease Turnover

Norman is the foreman of a machine shop. He has twenty-two men under his supervision. Early one rainy morning, he notices Pat, an employee of about two months, seated at his machine but not working. He says nothing, walking on. As he returns, Pat is still sitting at the machine and still not working.

Norman: (Sarcastically) I take it you don't feel like working today!

Pat: No, I don't! How about giving me the morning off?

Norman: You've got your nerve. I have half a mind to fire you.

Pat: Well, if that's the way you feel about it, why don't you?

Norman: Pick up your check—you're through!

PROBLEM

Norman was sarcastic in his approach, and Pat's retort was insubordinate. Neither got anywhere with this conversation. This sarcasm and lack of concern combined to irritate Pat, and that was that! The real problem was never discussed—*why* Pat didn't feel like working. Cost of turnover is high. How can Pat be saved from being fired?

ALTERNATE APPROACH

Norman: (Sarcastically) I take it you don't feel like working today!

Pat: Ease off, will you, Norman? No, I don't feel like working today. How about giving me the morning off?

Norman: Just like that? Maybe you should take the morning off, Pat. But can you tell me why you don't feel like working?

Pat: Yeh, it's my hand. I don't know what's wrong with it. This new job operation I'm on is really putting a cramp in my fingers. Today's damp weather makes it worse. My whole hand aches. I can't make it do what I want it to with this machine.

Norman: Have you been to the infirmary?

Pat: No, but maybe I should have them look at it. It just started bothering me since I went to work on this machine.

Norman: Is there something about the operation that's giving you trouble?

Pat: Yeh, it's this lever here. When I pull it across like this, it's really backward to the way my wrist and fingers would usually move.

Norman: I'd never noticed. Let me try it. By gosh, maybe you're right. It seems backward to normal movement. I'll talk with the engineer about it. Maybe we can do something so movement will be easier for you. Why don't you go to the infirmary now and see if they can relieve the soreness in your hand? Come back and let me know how you feel.

Pat: Thanks. I don't mean to goof you on rate, but I can't work right with this pain. I'll be back as soon as I can.

EVALUATION

Norman *focused on the problem*. In so doing, another problem surfaced. The obvious problem was Pat's sore hand. The *real* problem was, what had caused it.

To have replaced Pat would have cost both time and money. In addition, if the machine operation can be simplified, it should allow Pat to produce more. It could increase his job efficiency, too.

Get the total picture, then isolate the specific ingredients through dialogue. In the case of *Decrease Turnover*, the problem is production lag. But we need to know more:

1. What's the cause of the lag?
2. How great is the lag?
3. Who is causing it?
4. Why is it happening?
5. When did it begin?

This is getting to specifics, as Norman did. It's incomplete to stop with the general problem. Pinpoint the specific details. Only then is it possible to attempt a valid approach to a solution.

State the purpose of dialogue

When you initiate conversation, tell the purpose of the discussion as near the beginning as possible. This says to the other person you aren't there to waste time. It gives him a feeling of importance. It tells him you feel sufficiently comfortable with him to come right to the point.

There are two basic feelings in the other person that will urge him to join in open discussion: (a) the feeling that he can trust you, and (b) the feeling that you trust him.

One way to stifle these participative attitudes and to evoke feelings of distrust is to ask questions without telling why you want the information. The other person is apt to become suspicious quickly. This point becomes obvious in the following case:

Case Study No. 35 / "I wonder what he really means by that?"

Jeff Hefflin is the sales manager for a small tool and die company. He calls in one of his salesmen, Art Rogers.

Jeff: Come in, Art. Nice day, isn't it?

Art: Yes, I guess so.

Jeff: How have you been doing recently?

Art: OK, I guess.

Jeff: Do you like your job here, Art?

Art: Yes, I guess so.

Jeff: How's your production been?

Art: OK.

Jeff: Are you satisfied with your territory?

Art: Sure.

Jeff: Do you get along with your customers?

Art: No problem.

Jeff: Do you think you can improve your sales?

Art: Say, Jeff, what the hell do you want to know? All of these questions? You make me uncomfortable. *I'd* like to know what *you really* want to know!

PROBLEM

This series of questions would arouse suspicion from anyone, suspicion as to Art's real motives for this conference. Art hasn't stated the purpose of the meeting.

ALTERNATE APPROACH

Jeff: Come in, Art. I'm in the process of reviewing progress and potentials. Your record looks damned good again this year. But you know how I am, if there's anything we can do to help you to increase production, I'm open to suggestions.

Art: Well, now that you put it that way, I've never understood why you don't re-align that northern tip of the territory. There are several accounts I could call on while I'm up there and not have Tom making a special trip. One day would just about do it. Then, I'd give Tom some of the western part that takes extra mileage for me to cover. It'd about equal out for both Tom and me. Let's face it, we can use the time we save traveling to make sales.

Jeff: Good suggestion! Why don't you and Tom talk and I'll investigate the possibility right away? I hear you saying, too, that you'd like to increase your sales.

Art: You bet. And right now or I can't get the new boat I want by this summer.

Jeff: Let's see how I can help you.

Art: If you can give us support in some of the local papers it would help. I get better results after an advertising campaign in that media.

Jeff: I'll bring it up at our next advertising meeting and see about some budget re-allocation.

Art: While you're there, ask about those new charts, will you? We were supposed to get them several months ago. We've all been waiting. I think they'd be a real help when we don't carry samples. They'd do better than just words to make the sales.

Jeff: These are all good suggestions, Art. Any other ideas?

Art: One, and this is important. Several of us have wondered, when's the contest? I admit, when I see some of those prizes I try harder. Why not? It's great to get something extra, especially when I get extra commissions for doing it.

Jeff: The contest's coming up! Within three weeks we'll have the qualification rules published. With your attitude and spirit, Art, I have an idea you'll be one of our top qualifiers.

Anytime you have these things on your mind—suggestions like you've just made—come in and let's talk them. You've given me a lot of good ideas. I'll take a look at the territory, check on getting advertising support for you, see about the charts—and, the contest! Thanks, Art.

EVALUATION

Several suggestions came from this meeting because Jeff immediately stated the purpose of his meeting. He wasn't out to create suspense, so, he made his opening statement one to clarify "why" the meeting. This opening statement gave Art the feeling he was trusted, that Jeff valued his opinion and thinking in requesting his ideas. This gave him confidence to open up and share his thinking with Jeff.

Why not make conversations as mutually comfortable as possible? It's much easier to accomplish this when we state what we're talking about at the beginning, when we focus on the problem. We can unintentionally throw the listener off the scent of what we're talking about if we aren't careful. When problems are pressing on our minds, they can jam our talk-mechanism so that we virtually won't make sense to our listeners. It requires an astute listener to recognize this type of situation and be able to handle it properly. The following case exemplifies this:

Case Study No. 36 / What will they ever do without me?

Ronald Anderson is the national sales manager for a specialty paper company. He has some 1720 men nationwide, under his direction. He's with the company for twenty-six years now and is near retirement. He's lunching in the executive dining room of the home office with his president, Harper Taylor. The two men are good friends.

Ronald: There's nothing new on this stupid menu. Always the same thing every day. Why don't we get them to change menus once in awhile?

Harper: What the heck's wrong with you, Ronald? They never have the same menu two days in succession. You've been damned irritable lately. What's wrong?

Ronald: Nothing's wrong, Harper. And that's why I think it's a shame they're sending me out to pasture so soon.

Harper: You're just feeling sorry for yourself, Ronald. Forget it, you'll get along OK. Let's order.

PROBLEM

Failure to focus on the *real* problem. In addition, Harper isn't recognizing the frustration and personal feelings that are going on with Ronald at this crucial time.

ALTERNATE APPROACH

Ronald: There's nothing new on this stupid menu. Always the same thing every day. Why don't we get them to change menus once in awhile.

Harper: What the heck's wrong with you, Ronald? They never have the same menu two days in succession. You've been damned irritable lately. What's wrong?

Ronald: Nothing's wrong, Harper. And that's why I think it's a shame they're sending me out to pasture so soon.

Harper: Let's talk about that, Ronald. How do you feel about taking retirement later this year?

Ronald: I'm pretty upset about it, if you want to know the truth.

Most of the guys out there, I've hired myself. We're all friends. We've been a great team. I'll be honest with you, I don't know what they'll do without me. I'm not irreplaceable, I know that, but we've been friends and buddies, and we've produced!

Harper: You'll miss their friendship and being in on the action.

Ronald: You bet I will. Why, I could go across this country and never have to stay in a single hotel room if I didn't want to. I've got that kind of friends among the salesmen. I know all of them by name. Every one of them, and their families, too.

Harper: You're going to feel isolated.

Ronald: Yes, I'll be isolated from long-time friends. We've watched this company grow together, and together we've made it grow. Now I have to leave all that. Just shut the door on it and be dead to everyone. I don't think I can take it.

Harper: Why do you see it as isolation, Ronald?

Ronald: Why, because I'll be alone. My replacement will be the guy who contacts the salesmen. He'll be the man the salesmen look to for guidance. He'll be the one who gets the applause after his speeches at their meetings. I'll just be part of the past!

Harper: What are you going to do when you leave here, Ronald?

Ronald: I've told you, Harper, I'm going to move to Florida. I haven't decided just what I'll do. Probably catch up on my golf and fishing and sunshine.

Harper: What I hear you saying, Ronald, is that you don't intend being associated with many other people. You aren't talking about anything where you'll be leading.

Ronald: That's the way it stands now. What are you getting at?

Harper: What you've been telling me is, the reason you'll miss your job so much is that you'll miss the personal contact with the salesmen?

Ronald: Right!

Harper: If you had contact with another group of people where you'd be working toward a common goal, like increasing sales here, how would you feel about that?

Ronald: Pretty good! That may be what I need. I've got to have a goal to work toward.

Harper: And people to work with!

Ronald: Yes, yes, you're right. It wouldn't be so bad if I could get a group together and make something happen. It would be a great challenge to take something someone else says can't be done and make it happen.

Harper: I wish you could see your enthusiasm right now. All you need is a goal to work toward, a challenge to meet. Whoever said retirement says a person shouldn't work at something besides leisure?

Ronald: You're right again! Who says I have to just golf and fish? Why, I've got a helluva lot of good years ahead of me where I can develop new ideas and products and make things happen. I've just been feeling sorry for myself, and not thinking about doing something productive with my life.

Harper: Lots of men have two complete careers in their business lives. Look at a military man; he can have two careers and sometimes more. Why can't you!

Ronald: That's the way I'm going to start thinking. I'll look into the local Florida market and see if I can't find something that's attractive to me.

I'm hungry. Why don't we order?

EVALUATION

Through careful questioning, Harper led Ronald to see that his real problem was the need to be working at something productively. Harper was understanding. He recognized Ronald's need for something to replace the "stroking" he got from his salesmen, that fish and golf balls aren't the answer. He wasn't solicitous, nor did he disregard Ronald's feelings, To the contrary, he respected them.

Red flags of dialogue

What are some of the red flags of dialogue that can impair its real meaning and bring it to an impasse that prevents the possibility of reaching either the problem or a solution? These are red flags of dialogue:

> "I'd rather not discuss it."
> "Oh, nothing! Nothing's wrong!"
> "That's all right. It doesn't matter."
> "Let's not talk about it."
> "Don't worry about me. I'll be all right."

"There's nothing else to say."

"You just don't understand."

"There's no point in discussing it any further."

These are a sampling of the red flags in dialogue that signal frustration on the part of the speaker, and block the possibility of focusing on the problem.

What is frustration? It's the result of being unable to attain a specific goal. It's the result of a road block, a barrier that's thrown in the path of progress toward accomplishment of a particular goal or project, or the satisfaction of a certain important need.

Is it possible for conversation to continue when someone throws up one of these red flags? The normal impulse would be to say: "To hell with you! If that's the way you feel about things, I don't want to talk about it either!"

If we recognize that the cause for the flags is frustration, then we can deal with it on a more objective, satisfactory level.

Assume you're faced with someone who has just squelched you with the statement, "Let's not talk about it!" Of these three alternatives, which would you employ?

1. Change the subject.

2. Find out the cause.

3. Talk about it later.

To relieve tensions, step two would be the most effective approach. One and three would relieve tension temporarily, *maybe*, but the root cause would still exist. Let's analyze, however, what we could do with each of the three alternatives.

1. If you change the subject without acknowledging the statement at all, that's as good as saying, "I'm not listening to what you were saying." At least you're complying with the request. You aren't arguing it out, or worse yet, retaliating with a threat.

2. In your attempt to find out what caused this statement, recognize whatever feelings are associated with it. If they're of frustration, then your reply might be, "I hear lots of frustration in that statement; can you tell me what's causing this feeling?" You have recognized the feelings and are respecting them, yet asking for clarification so you can uncover the real problem.

3. To talk about it later, you allow the cause to continue, perhaps to intensify and distort.

What should our attitude toward problems be? To many of us, they are unwelcome, and we resent having to be involved with them. Perhaps we can take a different slant on this thinking if we heed the advice of Dr. Norman Vincent Peale:

> Don't fight a problem. And never complain when a problem strikes you. Instead, start asking questions of the problem. For it is full of know-how for you. Actually, a problem is one of God's greatest methods for teaching you, for helping you to develop.
>
> Charles F. Kettering, famous research scientist, was a wise man, a kind of natural-born philosopher. He was an inventive genius of high order, especially in the automotive field. I had a most illuminating conversation with this great thinker in the course of which he expounded his philosophy on problems. "I could do nothing without problems," he declared emphatically, "they toughen my mind. In fact," he said, "I tell my assistants not to bring me their successes, for they weaken me; but rather to bring me their problems, for they strengthen me."[29]

The wrap-up

To be meaningful, it's imperative that effective dialogue reach some conclusion, or at least an understanding, for the participants. Inconclusive dialogue results in frustration, anxiety, confusion, and irritation. To conclude the exchange of dialogue successfully, we must seek solutions and a path of action. Paraphrased, what we're saying is, we have to make a decision and establish a course to implement our decision. For many, this is difficult. We have a habit of procrastination when it comes to making a decision. Dr. Charles Mayo of the Mayo Clinic once stated in an interview that he'd never known anyone to die from overwork, but that he'd known lots of them to die from indecision. This says, it's wise to make the decision, regardless. It might be wrong, but at least it's a decision!

Too often we make a hasty decision that's based on the first problem presented. We should probe for the seat of the trouble or the cause of the problem. Find the right questions instead of quickly giving an answer. Probe deeply for the real problem. When you find the *real* problem, you'll usually find its solution with it. Then attempt making your decision as deftly and swiftly as possible.

Most of our energy is spent, daily, in seeking solutions. As managers, we make decisions on large and small matters—problems.

But wherever possible, as quickly as possible, *we must make decisions*. The nature of indecisiveness is unsettling to us and others who might be involved in the problem. *Do something, anything, only do something!*

Often we must resolve a decision before we have all of the facts. This produces feelings of uncertainty for many. This happens in business, in politics, signing a petition, etc., but we must be able to accept the fact there's not always absolute certainty. Therefore, our decision must be made by ascertaining the degree of probability involved. There's the possibility of being wrong, but there's the possibility of being right. The most valid fact is that you've made a choice. Only then can action begin to effect change.

When we seek a workable agreement for a pattern of action, we're not saying that all parties involved must be 100 percent in mutual agreement. In fact, 100 percent would probably indicate an undesirable situation. What we're striving for is to reach a conclusion for an action pattern that's acceptable to the participants in the dialogue. The goal of the action is to produce desired results that will be beneficial to the common objective.

Each problem will have variables relative to itself and can't be resolved by a pat, absolute answer. *There are no pat answers* because no two people see things the same way since no two people are alike in background and thinking. According to Ruell L. Howe in *The Miracle of Dialogue:*

> A person creatively participating in dialogue is one who has convictions, but they are convictions that genuinely relate to his basic character. He is also one who recognizes and accepts the convictions of others; indeed invites them to reveal them. All of us need the experience of living with people who speak out of the dpths of their beliefs and stand for them with courage. One needs to accept the challenge of another's thought or questions and come to terms with the boundaries and limitations that other peoples' point of view impose upon him. Such a person is a growing person who helps others grow with him. Indeed, we all gain power as persons when, in dialogue with others, we state our convictions, and they in turn, challenge or affirm us.[30]

It's wasted motion to attempt getting pat answers to questions. *It's necessary to listen to different points of view and seek different paths for action*, then conclude which approach is to be used, having as alternatives some of the other suggestions offered.

In concluding a dialogue session, the manager or leader should:

1. Re-state the problem in its entirety. This should be a re-statement of needs and/or problems, including the superficial, symptomatic problems and the real underlying one.

2. The manager should feed back the causes for the problem as stated during the dialogue, or e may ask the other person, or someone of the group, to feed back the causes.

3. The manager should ask for a summary here. Rather than give the summary, he should employ questions to elicit feedback from the other person, or group. In this way, he's sure that all understand what's being said. He should ask for summary on the areas of problems, agreement, disagreement, and what action is suggested to be taken. The more definitive the summary, the more apt it is to be understood and remembered. It's another form of repetition and a mandatory step in the wrap-up process.

4. The leader/manager should ask for amendments to what has been stated so far, and/or added thinking regarding the material presented. If the leader refuses to share the making of the decision with others, he fails to develop others and eventually loses the quality of suggestions made. Others soon cease offering suggestions that get turned down. A second-best decision that's accepted by most of the group might prove more productive than one the manager thinks is great but the group dislikes. *The success of decisions depends on both quality and acceptability.*

5. The manager will review the proposed course of action, being specific in his detail for procedure. Who does what, when, where, why, and how!

6. The manager now concludes the wrap-up by stating details for continued meeting, future meetings, reminders, and so forth.

The dialogue is dismissed.

7. The manager then evaluates himself, his dialogue, what he feels his strengths and weaknesses were, how he might improve his dialogue in the future. He must be as objective as possible in this evaluation. He can profit from each encounter with another human being if he's able to stand back from the meeting and honestly see what his strengths and weaknesses were. In this way, he can grow and mature to improve his future dialogues.

Effective dialogue concludes with mutual understanding between the people involved. Dialogue should yield a workable agreement for a pattern of action, and leave the door open for the pursuit of future dialogue.

Conversation isn't always easy and comfortable, but it's the main avenue available to a manager whereby he can relate successfully with his employees. Dialogue is a two-way street and must be participated in by both parties with equal enthusiasm and understanding. We must learn the needs and interests of others and talk in terms of these needs and interests. We uncover these factors through asking questions, effective listening, and acknowledgment. Good dialogue can establish and preserve a more pleasant and rewarding relationship for the manager with his employees. Judiciously used, it can decrease turnover and increase profits.

The successful manager learns to keep open the lines of communication with his subordinates, his peers, and his superiors. In this way he is able to develop understanding and locate problems. As a result of virile dialogue, the manager is better equipped to help his personnel become more successful and accomplish the overall objectives of the company.

REFERENCES

1. Rogers, Carl: *Client Centered Therapy.* Houghton, Mifflin, Boston, 1951.
2. Tournier, Dr. Paul: *To Understand Each Other.* John Knox Press, Richmond, Va., 1969.
3. Champion John M. and Bridges, Francis J.: *Critical Incidents in Management.* Richard D. Irwin, Inc., Homewood, Ill., 1969.
4. Rogers, Carl: *Client Centered Therapy.*
5. Planck, R. W.: "Should You Put the Office Grapevine to Work?" *Modern Office Procedures,* January, 1971.
6. Morrow, Dr. Alfred J.: *Behind the Executive Mask.* American Management Association, Inc., New York, 1964.
7. Maslow, Dr. Abraham: *Motivation and Personality.* Harper & Row, New York, 1954.
8. Herzberg, Frederick: *The Motivation to Work.* John Wiley & Sons, Inc., New York, 1959.
9. Townsend, Robert: *Up the Organization.* Alfred A. Knopf, New York, 1970.
10. Morrow, Dr. Alfred J.: *Behind the Executive Mask.*
11. Ibid.
12. Maslow, Dr. Abraham: *Motivation and Personality.*

13. Blake, Robert R. and Mouton, Jane S.: *The Managerial Grid*. Gulf Publishing Co., Houston, 1964.
14. Schmidt, Warren H. and Tannenbaum, Robert: "Management of Differences"; *Harvard Business Review*, Nov., Dec., 1960.
15. Fromm, Erich: *The Art of Loving*. Harper & Row, New York, 1956.
16. Liebman, Joshua: *Peace of Mind*. Simon & Schuster, New York, 1946.
17. Schmidt, Warren H. & Tannenbaum, Robert: "Management of Differences."
18. Herzberg, Fredrick: *The Motivation to Work*.
19. Giberson, Dr. Lydia: "What an Executive Should Know About Himself." Dartnell Corp., Chicago, 1964.
20. Maslow, Dr. Abraham: *Motivation and Personality*.
21. O'Connor, Dr. R. B.: "Your Emotions Can Be Contagious." *Supervisory Management*, 4:3, New York, 1959.
22. Russell, Bertrand: *The Autobiography of Bertrand Russell*. Little, Brown, Boston, 1967.
23. Nirenberg, Dr. Jesse S.: *Getting Through to People*. Prentice Hall, Englewood Cliffs, N.J., 1963.
24. Ibid.
25. Fromm, Erich: *The Art of Loving*.
26. Ibid.
27. Moore, Robert E.: *The Human Side of Successful Communication*. Prentice Hall, Englewood, N.J., 1961.
28. Likert, Rensis: *The Human Organization*. McGraw Hill, New York, 1967.
29. Peale, Dr. Norman Vincent: *You Can Overcome Any Problem*. Foundation for Christian Living, Pawling, N.Y., 1971.
30. Howe, Ruell L.: *The Miracle of Dialogue*. The Seabury Press, Inc., New York, 1963.